Praise for *The Little Picnic Book*

"There's no one else I'd go to for advice on creating the best picnic setup than the Picnic Queen herself. From choosing the right picnic basket to yummy recipes to listing every single item you need to bring, Cristina has you covered!"

—Allie Tong, @allie.eats

"You can count on Cristina's book for endless inspiration. She has a natural eye for art and design. There are so many wholesome recipes to take your picnic to the next level."

—Ally Chen, @fashionbyally

"A cookbook as whimsical and charming as it is informative and inspiring. With a mix of inventive recipes and fresh takes on the classics, it's a must for picnic enthusiasts and picnic newbies alike. After the expert packing tips and playful dish ideas, I'm eagerly planning my next picnic!"

—Kennedy Rose, @cozy.games

"Who said fancy picnics are only for influencers? Cristina Viseu's guide is about to make your life like a romance anime, one picnic at a time."

—Meilyne Tran, food streamer/COO and founder of GeexPlus

"*The Little Picnic Book* is the perfect guide to create your next aesthetically pleasing picnic experience. From delicious recipes to packing tips, this guide will help bring your picnics to the next level."

—Michael Tran, @BetweenSpoonfuls

"With practical advice and gorgeous photos, this book is a must-have for any picnic lover or coffee-table book enthusiast."

—Emily Bushman, author of *Bake Anime*

The Little
Picnic Book

The Little Picnic Book

A Cottagecore Picnic Guide

CRISTINA VISEU

CORAL GABLES

Copyright © 2024 by Cristina Viseu.
Published by Mango Publishing, a division of Mango Publishing Group, Inc.

Cover Design: Andrea Reza
Cover Photo/illustration: Cristina Viseu
Layout & Design: Andrea Reza & Elina Diaz

Mango is an active supporter of authors' rights to free speech and artistic expression in their books. The purpose of copyright is to encourage authors to produce exceptional works that enrich our culture and our open society.

Uploading or distributing photos, scans or any content from this book without prior permission is theft of the author's intellectual property. Please honor the author's work as you would your own. Thank you in advance for respecting our author's rights.

For permission requests, please contact the publisher at:
Mango Publishing Group
2850 S Douglas Road, 2nd Floor
Coral Gables, FL 33134 USA
info@mango.bz

For special orders, quantity sales, course adoptions and corporate sales, please email the publisher at sales@mango.bz. For trade and wholesale sales, please contact Ingram Publisher Services at customer.service@ingramcontent.com or +1.800.509.4887.

The Little Picnic Book: A Cottagecore Picnic Guide

Library of Congress Cataloging-in-Publication number: 2023951110
ISBN: (hc) 978-1-68481-441-1, (pb) 978-1-68481-442-8, (e) 978-1-68481-443-5
BISAC category code: CKB133000, COOKING / Picnicking & Tailgating

Printed in the United States of America

To my husband, Aaron, for believing in all my dreams.

Table *of* Contents

Intro: My Picnic Journey 13

What to Bring on a Picnic 17
Invite 18
Decoration Ideas 20
Menu 22
Food 24
The Picnic Blanket 26
A Small Table 27
Dishware 28
Glassware 30
Cutlery 31
Other essentials 32
How to Transport Your Food 35
How to Choose & Pack a Picnic Basket 40
A Bit *About* Oils 44
Grains 46
Pastas 48
Breads 50

Platters 53
Cheeseboard 55
Easy Introductory Cheese Pairings *and* Accompaniments 58
Crudité Board 65
Grazing Board 70
Fresh Fruit 73

Appetizers 75
Bruschetta 77
Melon Prosciutto Skewers 79

Croquettes ... 81
Fresh Spring Rolls ... 82
Fried Chicken Bites ... 84
Miso Chicken Skewers ... 86
Glazed Tteokbokki Skewers ... 88
Spicy Shrimp Kebabs ... 91
Pork and Green Onion Pan-Fried Dumplings ... 93
Pork and Chive Baos ... 97

Side Dishes ... 101

Grilled Vegetables ... 102
Enoki Mushroom Beef Rolls ... 105
Fried Tempura ... 107
Tonkatsu ... 110

Salads ... 113

Fruit Salad ... 115
Peach Burrata Salad ... 117
Yuzu Cabbage Salad ... 118
Simple Tangy Potato Salad ... 120
Roasted Root Vegetable Salad ... 122
Rice Noodle Salad ... 125
Fresh Lotus Root Salad ... 126
Caprese Salad ... 128
Pesto Pasta Salad ... 130
Lemon Pasta Salad ... 133

Rice *and* Noodles ... 135

Kimbap ... 137
Soothing Mushroom Rice ... 141
Onigiri ... 143
Spicy Tuna Onigiri ... 145
Salted Salmon Onigiri ... 146

Ume Onigiri 149
Inari Sushi 150
Easy Japchae 152

Sandwiches *and* Wraps **155**
Smoked Salmon Bagel *with* Lox *and* Cream Cheese 157
Cucumber Tea Sandwich 159
Katsu Sandwich 160
Japanese Egg Sandwich 163
Ham and Cheese Croissant 165
Caprese Sandwich 167
Prosciutto, Fig, *and* Brie Sandwich 169
Strawberry Cream Sandwich 171
Mini Focaccia Pizzas 172
Mini Puff Pastry Bites 175

Desserts **177**
Cherry Pie 179
Fruit Tarts 183
Croffles *with* Whipped Cream Cheese *and* Strawberries 187
Chocolate Strawberries 191
Lemon Tart 192
Strawberry Waffles 194
Zesty Lemon Pound Cake 196
Mini Strawberry Cakes 199
Strawberry Tanghulu 203
Dango 206
Floral Sugar Cookies 209

Beverages **211**
Sparkling Green Grape Ade 213
Spiced Cider 215
Strawberry Mint Spritz 217

Peach Bellini 219
Sparkling Lemonade 221
Strawberry Matcha Latte 223
Rosemary Grapefruit Sparkler 225
Strawberry Milk 227
Ginger Peach Tea 229
Sparkling Pear Green Tea Lemonade 230
Taro Milk Tea 233

Goodbye for Now 235
Thank You 236
About the Author 237

Intro: My Picnic Journey

As the sun began to dip below the horizon, we spread out our gingham blanket and set down the picnic basket in a clearing surrounded by tall trees. Above us, the leaves rustled in the gentle breeze and a symphony of birdsong echoed. It felt as though we had stepped into a different world—one where time seemed to stand still. We opened the basket and eager anticipation filled the air as we pulled out each dish, one by one. In the soft glow of the setting sun, everything looked even more beautiful. It was a perfect afternoon—one that I will always remember.

When I landed my dream job in the heart of downtown, I was ecstatic. I threw myself into my work, relishing the challenges and the long hours. But as the years passed, I began to feel restlessness gnawing at me. I grew tired of the noise and the crowds, yearning for a life that was slower and quieter.

And that was when I discovered picnicking. I grew accustomed to eating my meals at my desk. But one sunny autumn day, I decided to have a picnic with a friend in the park. It was the first of mine, and I will never forget that picnic. There is something magical about picnics. Perhaps it is the simple act of enjoying a meal outdoors, surrounded by nature. Or maybe it is the opportunity to slow down and savor the moment, free from the pressures of daily life.

I started sharing my picnics online and was pleasantly surprised at how many enjoy picnicking as much as I do. And as the little picnic club (my pet name for all those who enjoy picnics) grew, I decided it was about time to compile all the recipes and tips into a book.

There's nothing more satisfying than creating delicious meals from scratch and enjoying them in the sun, and this collection of recipes provides just that! The recipes are meant to be easy to follow even for novice or nervous cooks. If you feel the need to substitute—please do! This book is meant to be a very gentle guide.

Cooking is all about playing around with ingredients and flavors, taking risks and letting your imagination run wild; it should feel fun. The same goes for picnicking.

What to Bring on a Picnic

The *Invite*

Crafting an invitation for a picnic can be a thrilling experience. An effective invitation will set the tone for the entire affair and leave every guest eager to attend. It also provides context on how to dress, where to meet, and what to expect. In the digital age, a simple text to your guests will do for casual affairs. For something more formal, you can get creative with a physical card.

Steps

Step 1: Select a style and color that reflects the atmosphere of your gathering. You can also choose a theme and match the invite to that specific mood.

Step 2: Add a personal touch with maybe a hand-drawn illustration or an inside joke. For those who are keen in the art of graphic design, this is your time to shine. And for those who are not familiar, this might be an opportunity to experiment and get creative. Infuse your invitation with evocative words that will bring anticipation to those receiving it.

Step 3: Ensure all the necessary details are reflected in the invite. Time, place, and attire are the most notable ones. Additional information regarding parking and transportation would help the guests immensely. Remember to make it as easy as possible for your guests to attend your picnic function.

Step 4: Decorate the card and envelope.

Decoration *Ideas*

Stamps: Using stamps is a fun way to bring a touch of vintage charm to your invitation. You can use rubber stamps to add designs or messages. This gives it a whimsical and traditional feel, making your guests feel like they're receiving a personalized postcard from a loved one.

Twine: Another easy invite motif you can add is twine, which adds a rustic and earthy vibe to your invitation. You can use twine to tie your invitation cards together or wrap it around the invites, giving them a natural and effortless feel. You can even attach a small flower or leaf to the twine, adding a pop of color and a personalized touch.

Wax seals: Wax stamps have a timeless, classic feel that can make your invitation feel extra special. You can choose from a variety of designs, including traditional monograms, floral patterns, and fun shapes. To use a wax stamp, simply melt the wax over the closed envelope flap and press the stamp onto the melted wax. The result is a beautiful, personalized seal that adds a touch of elegance to your invitation.

Stickers: These are a fun and affordable way to add color and personality to your picnic party invitation. Choose stickers that match your party theme, such as a picnic basket or a cute little bee, to create a cohesive and festive look. You can even add a sheet of stickers to each invitation so your guests can use them to decorate their own picnic gear.

Ribbon: This is another lovely addition that can add a touch of elegance to your picnic party invitation. Choose a ribbon that matches your party colors or adds a pop of contrast. You can tie a bow or knot with the ribbon, or even weave a lace ribbon through the invitation to create a pretty border.

Hand-Drawn Illustrations: If you are artistic, consider drawing a few illustrations that match the theme of the picnic. You can also fill in the illustrations with watercolor.

Pressed or Dried Flowers: Pressed flowers are a beautiful and natural way to enhance your invitations. Simply collect a variety of flowers, leaves, and other plant materials from your garden or local park, press them between the pages of a heavy book for a few days, and then attach them to your invitations with a small dab of glue.

Washi Tape: Washi tape is also an excellent option for adding color and design to your invites. This versatile product comes in a wide range of vibrant colors and patterns, making it easy to customize your invites to match your picnic theme. Plus, because washi tape is low-tack, it can be easily removed and repositioned.

Fragrance: For an extra special touch, spray the card with a pleasant floral or earthy scent.

Menu

Menu

Starters:
- Garden Fresh Salad with Vinaigret*
- Heirloom Tomato Bruschetta
- Assorted Cheese and Charcuterie

Main Courses:
- Gourmet Chicken Sandwiches wi
- Vegan Quinoa
- Grilled Veggie Skewers with

Sides:
- Seasonal Fruit Medley
- Homemade Potato Salad
- Artisanal Bread Selection

Desserts:
- Mini Berry Tarts
- on Drizzle Cakes
- -Dipped Stra

When preparing for a picnic, one must take into account the menu, as well as the items needed to properly enjoy the meal.

To start, consider the season and adjust the menu accordingly; for instance, lighter dishes may be better suited during warmer months than in the wintertime. There are also certain ingredients that are more readily available in some seasons than others.

Next, take into account what type of event you're hosting—you should create a theme or focus to drive your menu choices. Consider the formality and kind of atmosphere you are looking to create; will it be a fancy multi-course meal, or more relaxed? Are you focusing on regional cuisine or lighter fare? Think about the balance of flavors and ingredients, as well as what will make the meal most special and memorable for your guests. You should also consider selecting dishes that can easily be transported.

Guests may have dietary restrictions or preferences that must be honored. I would highly recommend asking all the guests their restrictions and planning substitutions properly.

Also think about which flavors will work well together—while some variations may be unexpected, they can result in an enchanting and unforgettable dining experience. Lastly, always remember to make adjustments as necessary. It's always advantageous to be flexible, as you never know where the journey will guide you.

Food

For food, it is best to pack light fare that will not spoil in the heat and is easy to enjoy, such as fruits and sandwiches. However, don't be limited to just that. There are plenty of dishes suitable for picnicking.

Start by selecting dishes that complement each other's flavors and textures. I find it easiest to choose a theme or season and then a main dish. Once your main dishes have been chosen, fill out the rest of the menu with items that bring balance.

Ensure the bold flavors in one dish don't overpower subtle tastes in another. Consider the flavors and colors that your chosen items will bring to the table, and make sure they pair harmoniously. Don't forget to think about ingredients that are in season, as well as beverages that fit with the general theme. Creating a smooth flow between courses is essential for creating an enjoyable atmosphere; warm earthy tones brought on by appetizers make way for crisp refreshing cocktails. Rich hearty mains pair well with lighter, brighter side dishes.

Consider the travel time from your home to your picnic location as well. Longer travel times might require a cooler or ice packs for perishable goods. If the location is a trek away, consider how you will carry the items to your picnic location. Will you need a basket or a trolley?

The Picnic Blanket

Not all picnic blankets are created equal. The perfect fabric should be soft to keep you comfy, but also durable enough to stand up to any unexpected spills or muddy paws. It needs to be made of resistant materials so that it will last through multiple outings, yet remain light enough to be easily portable. The perfect picnic blanket should be able to resist water and dirt, while still maintaining its inviting character.

Be wary of light colors on fresh grass, as it will stain. Certain materials may get stained easily as they become exposed to the elements. This can be avoided by carefully choosing a patterned or darker-colored picnic blanket. If you are a fan of lighter-colored textiles, I would recommend layering two blankets—a waterproof one as a barrier and a softer, cozier one on top.

A Small Table

A picnic is not truly a picnic without a proper table on which to lay out the feast. However, lugging a heavy table through the park can be a real hassle. A small folding table is the perfect solution. It is light enough to carry without difficulty, yet large enough to provide a sturdy surface for plates and cups to rest on. You won't worry about your glass tumbling while you lie about. Best of all, it can be easily tucked away into a backpack or basket when the meal is finished.

A small table can be a lovely addition to any picnic spread. To make the most of this dainty piece of outdoor furniture, start by covering the table with a cheerful tablecloth. Then, arrange an assortment of fruits, cheeses, and other picnic snacks on small platters and plates. Glasses that are prone to tip over or cumbersome dishes can also rest on this table. For a finishing touch, add a few sprigs of flowers to the table.

Dishware

When hosting a picnic, the type of dishware you choose can set the tone and make an impression on your guests. It's important to choose dinnerware that stands out but also meets the needs of your event. Choosing the perfect dishware can be daunting, but when you're informed of your options, it becomes easy.

Paper

The lowest maintenance form of dishware is of course, disposable paper dishes! Cleanup is especially easy. Nowadays, most paper dishes come in a multitude of different designs. Paper dishes allow you to enjoy your picnic without having to worry about the dishes afterwards.

Plastic

Reusable plastic is gaining popularity for outdoor excursions especially for those with young children. Plastic dishware has one major advantage; they are typically not breakable or hard to break. Furthermore, they are wonderfully lightweight to carry and easy to store in your picnic basket or hamper.

Bamboo/Wood

Bamboo or wooden dishes for your outdoor event are not only an ecological choice, but also a beautiful one. Not only do wooden dishes possess a natural charm, but they also have their own rustic feel which adds more definition to your outdoor event.

Ceramic

Although heavier than the rest, ceramic dishes offer a touch of sophistication. They also offer another advantage—the ability to resist heat and chilly temperatures better than regular plastic or paper utensils.

Floral China

If you're looking to create an outdoor event that is sure to have your guests feeling like royalty, then you should consider investing in china for the occasion. Floral china exudes beauty and finesse, imparting a touch of luxury to an already special gathering. These stunning vessels are unfortunately quite fragile and often prone to breakage. Take care when transporting fine china.

Glassware

Make sure you choose a set of glassware that is reliable, robust and will endure whatever activities your picnic requires. Whether your gathering requires on-the-go sipping or something elegant for outdoor feasting, select a set of glasses with sturdy bases to avoid any precarious spills.

Shorter glasses do fare better on outdoor excursions. The taller the glass, the more delicate guarding it will need. Of course, having a table or flat surface for the glassware to rest on will open up more possibilities. Stemmed glasses do not rest easily on a grassy knoll.

In terms of interchangeability—it's easy to be flexible for glassware on a picnic. Wine glasses can double as water glasses and vice versa. Tea cups however should be reserved for tea or coffee.

Cutlery

When hosting a picnic, it is important to consider what type of cutlery to bring.

Stainless steel flatware is a popular choice for picnics, as it is durable and easy to clean. For a more elegant touch, you could opt for sterling silver flatware. Wood and bamboo are also popular choices for a more rustic feeling. Whatever type of flatware you choose, be sure to include enough forks, knives, spoons, and other necessary utensils for all of your guests. Don't forget tongs and special serving utensils as well. With the proper cutlery, your picnic will be sure to impress.

Other Essentials

To truly feel refreshed and rejuvenated in nature, however, it's important to first have all the essentials that will make your experience and cleanup effortless.

You'll want to make sure you bring napkins and/or wet wipes along; it'll save you from sticky fingers. A disposable garbage bag can help the area keep tidy. To protect yourself from the sun's powerful rays, make sure to bring sunscreen, and perhaps even a parasol or sunshade. Don't forget blankets and small pillows so that you can get comfortable, as well as bug spray should any pests come along.

With all these essentials taken care of, all that's left is to sit back, relax, and enjoy being surrounded by nature while making wonderful memories.

Picnic *Checklist*

- ☐ Picnic blanket
- ☐ Picnic basket
- ☐ Appetizer
- ☐ Main dish
- ☐ Dessert
- ☐ Beverages
- ☐ Garnish
- ☐ Dishes
- ☐ Cutlery
- ☐ Serving dishes
- ☐ Serving cutlery
- ☐ Glassware and straws
- ☐ Napkins

Optional Items

- ☐ Table
- ☐ Small pillows
- ☐ Blankets
- ☐ Bug spray if needed
- ☐ Parasol/sun shade/sunblock
- ☐ Florals
- ☐ Name cards for more formal affairs
- ☐ Menus for more formal affairs
- ☐ Food cover
- ☐ Corkscrew for wine

Easy Picnic Templates

Fancy Tea Party Picnic

Effort: high

Appetizer: cheeseboard

Main Course: an assortment of tea sandwiches

Dessert: cherry pie or small macarons

Beverage: tea with sugar and milk, champagne, or another sparkling beverage

Cutlery and plateware: floral plates with gold cutlery

Rustic Casual Picnic

Effort: low

Appetizer: fresh strawberries

Main Course: fig and prosciutto sandwiches

Dessert: fresh fruit tarts

Beverage: matcha latte

Cutlery and plateware: wood and ceramic plates with wooden cutlery

Sunset Picnic

Effort: medium

Appetizer: a light salad

Main Course: kimbap

Dessert: dango

Beverage: taro milk tea

Cutlery and plateware: gingham plates with plastic cutlery

How to *Transport* Your Food

To ensure that your delectable spread is in pristine condition as it transfers from your kitchen to the great outdoors, use these simple tips and tricks.

Start by narrowing down the selection of food you plan to bring, choosing items that are certain to travel well. Pack everything into reusable containers with an airtight seal, or cooler bags designed for keeping perishables chilled. Similar items should be grouped together. For example, there should be a designated fruit container and a designated dessert container. Sandwiches and delicacies can be wrapped with parchment paper or stored in a bag.

Foods at similar temperatures should also be packed next to each other. Some items are better assembled on-site and can provide an interactive experience for the guests.

Fruits: When it comes to transporting fruits, it's important to choose fruits that won't be easily squashed or bruised on the journey. Think apples, oranges, grapes, and strawberries. Pack the fruits in a sturdy container or basket, using paper towels or cloth to cushion them and prevent any unwanted jostling. You can still pack delicate fruits, such as peaches, but make sure there is no excess room in your container for movement. It's also a good idea to keep your fruits in a cool place, such as a cooler or insulated bag, to prevent them from getting too hot on the way.

Sandwiches: Sandwiches are a staple picnic food and can be easily transported in a sandwich container or wrapped in parchment paper and secured with twine. If possible, store sandwiches on their sides, so that the condiments do not leak onto the bread and create a soggy sandwich. Open-faced sandwiches can be assembled during the picnic to ensure that the ingredients stay fresh.

Salads: Salads are another delicious and healthy picnic option, but they can be a little more difficult to transport. To avoid any spills or leaks, pack your salad in a sturdy container with a tight-fitting lid. It's also a good idea to keep your salad dressing separate in a small container, adding it to the salad just before you're ready to eat.

Pasta or Noodle Salads: Pasta salads are great for picnics because they're easy to make and can be served cold. When transporting noodle salads, use a container with a tight-fitting lid and keep it in a cool place, such as a cooler or insulated bag. You can also add a little extra dressing to the noodles just before serving, to make sure they stay moist and flavorful. To prevent noodle salads from clumping, it is vital that the noodles are coated evenly in enough oil.

Meat Dishes: Transporting meat dishes for a picnic requires careful consideration to ensure that the meat stays fresh and safe to consume. For meats like chicken, pork, and beef, it is best to pack them in sealed containers that are leak-proof and airtight. This will help to keep them fresh and prevent any cross-contamination with other foods during transit. Enjoy the meat dishes early at the picnic to ensure freshness.

Baked Goods: For cookies, a flat container with a tight-fitting lid is ideal, as this will prevent them from shifting and getting crushed during transport. You can also use paper bags if you wrap them tightly. Lumpier goods like muffins or scones can be transported in a shallow container, or wrapped individually and placed in a deeper container to prevent them from toppling over. For savory baked goods such as quiches or pies, a deeper, covered dish is necessary to protect the delicate pastry crusts. Cakes and tarts should be stored in a cake box.

Boxed Lunches or Bentos: It's very easy to transport individual boxed lunches or bento boxes. Make sure that the box is closed tightly and secure a band over the box so the lid does not accidentally open. Use a piece of fabric or *furoshiki* to tie around the box for added security.

Beverages: When transporting different types of beverages such as tea and lemonade, it is essential to consider the type of container you are using. For hot beverages like tea, a thermos is an ideal choice as it will retain the heat and flavor for an extended period. For cold drinks like lemonade, a jug with a tight-fitting lid works wonders as it keeps the drink from spilling. Some cold drinks can be assembled at the picnic by transporting the syrup and garnish separately.

How to Choose & Pack a *Picnic Basket*

When you set out to choose your ideal picnic basket, there will be plenty of options. Think about how large a basket you will need, the handle, and if you need extra insulation. As you browse, take time to admire the intricate designs, artwork and embroidery crafted into each piece. When it comes down to it, choose one that works for you.

Packing your basket will feel extremely intuitive. However, here are some additional pointers should you need help.

The key to a balanced basket is in establishing the perfect foundation. It is important to start with the heavier items at the bottom so more fragile items can lay near the top. The bottom layer should consist of items like serving ware, plates, and jars.

Consider wrapping delicate items with napkins or padding with a blanket. Fine china should be wrapped individually. Secure cutlery together with a napkin or ribbon and tuck. Lighter fare such as salads, cut vegetables, cheese, and dessert should go on the top.

General Food *Safety* Tips

Before we get to the recipes, it's important to establish some general food safety tips.

There are a few guidelines to follow to ensure a delightful picnic experience. As you get ready to prepare your meals, know that the first step is food hygiene; it is important to wash hands with soap and water before cooking and handling food. When entering the kitchen, ensure any utensils to be used are clean, along with the surface area used for cutting boards and pans. Wash all fresh produce before you prep it for cooking or eating.

Don't cross-contaminate surfaces that come into contact with uncooked meats and eggs with any cooked or ready-to-eat food items. A handy tip is to designate separate cutting boards for raw meats and other produce that will be eaten raw, such as salad ingredients.

Food items need proper storage as well, stored either in the refrigerator or freezer to prevent bacteria from growing on perishable items. Ensure all foods are properly cooled before being placed in their containers and then sealed. Keep all perishable items chilled and out of the sun. Generally, most cooked food should not be left at room temperature longer than two hours, including transport time.

To keep pests away, consider putting food away when not nibbling, or covering it with a mesh cover.

A Bit *About* Oils

Cooking oils are great ingredients that can bring both texture and flavor to your dishes. But with the many types of oils available, it's important to know which oil performs best in different use cases. Smoke point is an important factor when choosing the right type of oil. This refers to the temperature at which an oil begins to break down and burn, leading to a smoky taste or smell.

Low-smoke-point oils (200–300°F or 100–150°C) are good for dressings, drizzling over cooked dishes, and marinades, while higher ones (400°F or 205°C) are great when you're pan-frying, stir-frying, or deep-frying. Each oil has its own flavor profile, which should also be taken into consideration when choosing your cooking oil!

Ultimately, choosing the right oil means ensuring it can handle the temperature you're cooking at and that the taste of the oil suits the recipe.

Grains

In this book, there will be some recipes that require knowing how to cook and choose various grains. From rice to pastas to bread, all of these will be important on our picnic adventure. Selecting the right grain for each recipe may require some trial-and-error experimentation, but learning the basics of buying and preparing will provide a solid foundation.

Rice

Not all rice is created equal. Factors such as flavor, texture, and cooking time can all be affected by the type of rice chosen for your dish. It is essential to have a thorough understanding of the different types of rice available and their unique characteristics. By doing so, you will be able to choose the perfect variety for your recipe.

Although there are no rules in cooking, here are some guidelines for how to use each rice. For sushi, onigiri, or kimbap, short-grain rice is the best choice, as it is sticky and holds together well. On the other hand, long-grain rice can be used to serve with side dishes due to its fluffy texture.

White vs Brown Rice

White rice is commonly polished and processed to remove the husk, bran, and germ. It has a mild flavor profile and a firm and dry texture. On the other hand, brown rice is unpolished and retains more nutrition than white rice. Brown rice has a nutty flavor and chewy texture due to its high fiber content. It also takes a bit longer to cook and some varieties may need to soak to cook thoroughly.

Long-Grain Rice

This type of rice is categorized by its slender grain shape. It's generally fluffy, but stiffer in texture, and used in dishes such as pilafs, stir-fries, or accompanying other savory side dishes. Common types of long grain are jasmine or basmati.

Short-Grain Rice

Short-grain rice has a more rounded grain shape and is characterized by its slightly chewy texture. This type of rice is commonly used in dishes such as sushi or congee. Short-grain rice is able to hold its shape well, even after being cooked and mixed with other ingredients.

Pastas

Pasta is one of the most beloved and widely consumed food products in the world, with a history dating back centuries. In fact, there are over two hundred distinct types of pasta shapes in existence, each with its own unique properties and best uses. Although I can't cover all the different shapes, here are a few popular ones to note. You can always use pastas interchangeably, but there are a few that I personally prefer.

Spaghetti is long, thin, and cylindrical in shape and you've most likely have had it before. It is typically made from durum wheat semolina and water, and is often paired with rich, hearty sauces such as Bolognese or carbonara. This versatile pasta is easy to cook and goes well with a range of ingredients.

Fusilli is a corkscrew-shaped pasta with a twisted spiral shape along the entire length of the noodle. The spiral shape of fusilli makes it fun and visually interesting.

Penne is another classic pasta shape that consists of short, cylindrical tubes with diagonal cuts on each end. This shape allows the pasta to hold onto sauces and other ingredients.

Rotini visually can look similar to fusilli at a glance. The main difference between rotini and fusilli is that rotini has a tighter coil with a sharp edge. Both are delicious and great in salads.

Farfalle is a delicate and delightful pasta that is shaped like a bowtie. The unique shape also makes farfalle a great choice for salads or dishes that require a touch of elegance and whimsy.

Rigatoni is a large, tubular pasta with a ridged surface that helps it hold onto sauce. It's regularly used in baked pasta dishes and with hearty meat sauces. Its size also makes it ideal for stuffing with cheese or other fillings. The sturdy shape also makes it a popular choice for dishes that require a substantial, chewy bite.

Linguine is similar to spaghetti, but its wider, flatter shape gives it a more elegant appearance. It's perfect for delicate sauces, like seafood or oil-based sauces, as it allows the sauce to evenly coat the pasta without overpowering it.

It's important to note that different types of pasta shapes serve different purposes. Whichever pasta you choose, I'm sure it will be just right.

Breads

Choosing the appropriate bread for a sandwich can elevate the taste experience from ordinary to extraordinary. Whether it is for a light and delicate tea sandwich, or a thick and delectable club sandwich, there are several options to ponder when selecting the right subset of breads. Sourdoughs lend an earthy wholesome flavor, while ciabattas provide rustic heartiness; choosing either can add unexpected zest to your menu. For those craving something with a subtle sweetness, wheat breads can provide crumbly texture as well as gentle flavor nuances; prepared properly, they make a delightful accompaniment to all varieties of fillings. Ultimately, selecting your ideal type of bread might come down to experimenting and sampling.

Brioche

Brioche is a type of bread that is made with eggs and butter, which gives it a rich and fluffy texture. It is often used for sweet dishes, such as French toast, but can also be used for savory dishes, such as egg sandwiches.

Ciabatta

Ciabatta is an Italian bread that has a chewy texture and large, irregular holes. It is often used as a filling appetizer or a side for soups.

Focaccia

Focaccia is an Italian bread that is similar to ciabatta in terms of texture and appearance. However, focaccia is typically seasoned with herbs, olive oil, and toppings. It is soft in appearance and texture.

Baguette

Baguettes are long, thin loaves of French bread that have a crispy crust and a soft interior. They are typically used for sandwiches that contain meat or cheese, as their thin shape makes them easy to eat on the go.

Sourdough

Sourdough bread is made with a starter culture of yeast and bacteria, which gives it a slightly sour and tangy flavor. It is often used for grilled cheese sandwiches or other types of sandwiches that benefit from its distinct taste.

Japanese Milk Bread

This bread, also known as *shokupan*, is a type of white bread that is popular in Japan for fruit sandwiches or egg sandwiches. The bread has a soft, fluffy texture. It's typically sliced thick and has a pleasant, slightly sweet taste.

Platters

Cheeseboard

Nothing says comfort like great cheese!

Constructing the perfect cheeseboard is an art form, and I'm here to teach you how to create an effortless cheeseboard for your next picnic. Trust me, your guests will be impressed!

Step One: Choose Your Cheese

The first step is to choose your cheese. When choosing your cheeses, think of contrast, color, flavor, and texture. Go for a mix of hard and soft cheeses. Some of my favorites include cheddar, Brie, parmesan, a sharp cheddar, Gouda, and goat cheese. If you're not sure what kind of cheese to get, your local produce store should have a cheese monger who can help you make the perfect selection.

When pairing cheeses, it's best to think of contrast. Pair soft cheeses with crisp crackers or a bright piece of pear. You also don't want to overwhelm any individual flavor, so I would typically advise against choosing two very strong cheese flavors together.

However, the sky's the limit, and there is no wrong way to do cheese!

Hard Cheeses

- Parmigiano-Reggiano (Parmesan)
- Pecorino Romano
- Cheddar
- Gouda
- Manchego
- Gruyère
- Asiago
- Comté

Soft Cheeses

- Brie
- Camembert
- Goat cheese (Chèvre)
- Feta
- Blue cheese (Roquefort, Gorgonzola, Stilton)
- Mozzarella
- Burrata
- Taleggio
- Cambozola
- Époisses

Semi-Hard Cheeses

- Gouda
- Fontina
- Havarti
- Muenster
- Raclette
- Provolone

Step Two: Choose Your Accompaniments

Now that you've got your cheese selection sorted, it's time to choose what you'll serve with it. Again, you'll want a mix of sweet and savory options. Some of my favorite accompaniments include fruit (fresh or dried), nuts, fig paste, olives, honey, crackers, and bread.

Dips

- Honey
- Fig paste
- Jams
- Balsamic glaze

Fruits & Sweets

- Pears
- Table grapes
- Apples
- Berries
- Figs
- Dried cherries
- Dark chocolate

Nuts/Crunchy Bits

- Macadamia
- Walnuts
- Almonds
- Marcona almonds
- Peanuts
- Pine nuts
- Cashews
- Pistachios

Pickles/Preserves

- Olives
- Capers
- Cornichons
- Pickled onions

Grains

- Crackers
- Crostini
- Breadsticks
- Water crackers
- Herb-infused crackers (rosemary, lavender, etc.)
- Multigrain crackers
- Sourdough

Step Three: Choose Your Garnish

It is essential to pay extra attention to the garnishes and herbs that you choose as finishing touches for your cheeseboard. Adding edible blooms can give the board an elegant aesthetic, while strategically arranged sprigs of herbs can contribute a touch of flavor and earthy appeal. Ultimately, garnishes should be hand-picked with care to harmoniously complement your delectable selection of cheeses.

Garnishes

- Sprigs of rosemary
- Lavender
- Edible wildflowers
- Chamomile buds
- Basil
- Thyme
- Chives

Easy Introductory Cheese Pairings and Accompaniments

In a pinch, here are some cheese pairings that are sure to please any palate! Remember, you can swap any ingredients to suit yourself and your guests.

Pairing 1: Rustic

A harmonious blend of bold and savory flavors, featuring Asiago, Gruyère, Pecorino Romano, and chèvre, paired with an array of rustic accompaniments.

- Asiago
- Gruyère
- Pecorino Romano
- Chèvre (goat cheese)
- Rosemary crackers
- Dry salami or prosciutto
- Pickled red onions
- Fig paste
- Fresh apple slices
- Dried figs or apricots
- Pistachios
- Garnish: Sprigs of sage

Pairing 2: Creamy Delight

Indulge in the luscious creaminess of Brie, Camembert, Manchego, and Gouda, enhanced by the perfect combination of sweet and savory elements.

- Brie cheese
- Camembert cheese
- Manchego cheese
- Gouda cheese
- Fresh baguette slices
- Prosciutto or sliced smoked salmon
- Fig jam or honey
- Sliced pears or grapes
- Toasted almonds
- Arugula or watercress
- Garnish: Sprigs of fresh thyme or rosemary

Pairing 3: Gourmet Trio

These exquisite cheeses provide a sophisticated and indulgent experience, beautifully complemented by an array of French-inspired accompaniments.

- Camembert cheese
- Comté cheese
- Roquefort cheese
- Baguette slices
- Sliced prosciutto or jambon de Bayonne
- Cornichons
- Dijon mustard
- Fig jam or fresh figs
- Walnuts or almonds
- Grapes
- Garnish: Fresh thyme sprigs

Transporting the Cheese and Serving Sizes

Transporting a cheeseboard requires some careful planning to ensure that all the delicious cheeses arrive at their destination in one piece. If you opt to place everything on the board, assemble it first and then carefully wrap the board so that the items don't shift. You can accomplish this with cling wrap or parchment paper. Make sure that you transport the board face up. Secure it tightly so it does not tilt during transit. Jams and items prone to spilling should be wrapped separately.

Alternatively, assemble the cheeseboard on-site to prevent any damage to the delicate components. Pack each item separately and use insulated containers to keep foods at the optimal temperature. This will require some prep time before eating. Wherever you assemble the board, make sure to carry it safely to avoid any accidents.

When it comes to selecting the right amount of cheese for your guests, there are a few things to keep in mind. Consider the duration of your event as well as other foods you will bring. On average, it's best to plan for about two to three ounces of cheese per person if you're offering a variety of cheeses as part of a larger spread. If you're serving cheese as part of a larger meal or appetizer, you may want to adjust the amount accordingly.

Crudité Board

Ah, the crudité platter. A picnic staple that is light, refreshing, and delicious. It's easy to make, convenient for snacking, and requires no cooking! But what is the secret to crafting the perfect crudité platter? Is it all about the vegetables? The dip? The presentation?

The answer is a little bit of all three.

Do choose a variety of colors and textures when selecting your vegetables. This will not only make for a beautiful display, but it will also ensure that there is something for everyone. Carrots, celery, radishes, bell peppers, cucumbers, cucumbers, peppers, cherry tomatoes, and snap peas are all great choices.

Make sure the vegetables are fresh. This sounds like a very obvious step, but the freshness of the vegetables really makes all the difference and is the most important tip for making a great crudité veggie platter. After all, you want your guests to enjoy eating the vegetables, not just looking at them! I like to shop for vegetables the morning of my picnic. Make sure to wash and chop the veggies just before you're ready to serve them.

Vegetable Suggestions

- Small carrots
- Celery
- Radishes
- Cherry tomatoes
- Bell pepper
- Cucumber
- Snap peas
- Cauliflower
- Broccoli

Dip Recipes

Don't forget the dip! The dip is the funnest part of the crudité platter, as it drastically changes the flavor and tone of the plate. I recommend a classic hummus, something a bit spicy, and a creamy dip to start.

Get creative with your presentation. Garnish with fresh herbs and flowers. This step is optional, but I think it really takes the platter to the next level. Some of my favorites for garnishing are parsley, basil, edible wildflowers, and chives.

Whether you're hosting a party or simply looking for a healthy snack option, a crudité platter is always a good idea. By following these simple tips, you'll be on your way to creating the perfect crudité platter in no time!

Each of the dips below makes two to three servings. You can alter based on your party size.

Dip 1: Classic Sour Cream

Ingredients:
1 tablespoon chopped fresh dill
1 tablespoon chopped fresh chives
½ cup sour cream
¼ teaspoon garlic powder
salt and pepper, to taste

Steps:

Step 1: Finely chop dill and chives.

Step 2: Add the sour cream, garlic powder, salt, and pepper to the bowl and stir well to combine.

Step 3: Add salt and pepper to taste.

Dip 2: Spicy Hummus

Ingredients:
¼ cup tahini
1 can chickpeas, drained and rinsed
2 tablespoons olive oil
1 tablespoon cold water
2 tablespoons lemon juice
2–3 cloves garlic, minced
¼ teaspoon red chili flakes
¼ teaspoon salt

Steps:

Step 1: To make the hummus, drain beans and rinse. Juice fresh lemons and set aside.

Step 2: Add the olive oil, tahini, lemon juice, garlic, red chili flake, cumin, salt, and beans in a food processor. Blend to a creamy consistency. Add cold water and continue blending until the mixture is smooth.

Dip 3: Roasted Red Pepper

Ingredients:
1 large red bell pepper
¼ cup chopped fresh parsley
¼ cup chopped fresh cilantro
½ cup plain Greek yogurt
1 tablespoon extra-virgin olive oil
1 tablespoon fresh lemon juice
½ teaspoon smoked paprika
¼ teaspoon cumin
salt and pepper, to taste

Steps:

Step 1: Preheat the oven to 425°F (220°C). Cut the red bell pepper into quarters and remove the stem and seeds. Place the pepper quarters on a baking sheet lined with parchment paper, skin side up.

Step 2: Roast the red pepper in the preheated oven for 15 to 20 minutes, or until the skin is charred and the flesh is tender. Remove the pepper from the oven and let it cool for a few minutes.

Step 3: Once the pepper has cooled, remove the charred skin and discard it. Add the chopped parsley, cilantro, Greek yogurt, olive oil, lemon juice, smoked paprika, cumin, salt, and pepper to the food processor with the roasted pepper.

Step 4: Blend the ingredients together until they are smooth and creamy. Taste the dip and adjust as necessary.

Grazing Board

Grazing boards have become incredibly popular, known for their sheer versatility as an all-in-one platter. The best thing about grazing boards is how easily customizable they are. Combine charcuterie, cheese, fresh fruits, vegetables, nuts, and accompaniments any way you like. They're the perfect appetizer or main course, offering a little bit of everything for everyone. Not only do they look visually stunning, but they also provide an array of flavors and textures that can fit any taste preference.

Ingredient Suggestions

Favorite assorted cheeses: cheddar, Brie, Gouda, Camembert, blue cheese, goat cheese
Favorite cured meats: prosciutto, salami, pepperoni, ham, mortadella
Crackers: water crackers, wheat crackers, or rice crackers
Fresh fruits: grapes, berries, sliced apples, or pears
Dried fruits: apricots, figs, dates, or raisins
Nuts: almonds, walnuts, cashews, or pistachios
Olives: kalamata olives, green olives, or stuffed olives
Bread or baguette slices
Assorted spreads: hummus, pesto, tapenade
Pickles or cornichons
Crudité: carrot sticks, cucumber slices, cherry tomatoes
Dips: spinach artichoke dip, or roasted red pepper dip
Antipasto: marinated artichokes, roasted peppers, or sun-dried tomatoes
Cheese straws or breadsticks
Honey or fruit preserves

How to Arrange

Step 1: Start by selecting a large board or platter to display your grazing board. Arrange the meats on the board in an attractive and visually pleasing manner.

Step 2: Fold the charcuterie. You can make charcuterie roses by laying salami or similar cured meat around a wine glass and inverting. You can also arrange in a fan-like pattern.

Step 3: Arrange the cheeses in clusters on the board. Cut some of them into bite-sized cubes and others in triangular thin pieces. Soft cheeses should remain intact.

Step 4: Surround the meats and cheeses with an assortment of crackers and breads. Add a variety of textures and shapes to create contrast. If there is not enough space on your board, you can opt to have the crackers and breads in their own bowl.

Step 5: Add fruits and vegetables to the board. Arrange in small clusters and fill in any empty spaces.

Step 6: Scatter nuts around the board or pour them into small ramekins. Mix and match different types of nuts to create an interesting flavor profile.

Step 7: Add small bowls of honey and fig jam to the board. These can be used as dips for the cheese and fruit.

Step 8: Finally, add any optional additions, such as olives or hummus. These can be placed in small bowls or directly on the board.

Fresh Fruit

A picnic is not a picnic without fruit. There's just something about the sweetness and juiciness of fruit that makes it the perfect companion for a day spent outdoors. Whether you're enjoying a long extended leisurely lunch in the park or a short picnic in the fields, fruit will help to fuel your body and keep you going.

Imagine a juicy orange, bursting with sweetness. Or a tart green apple, crisp and crunchy. Fruit is an essential part of any picnic. It's a healthy way to satisfy your sweet tooth, and it helps to keep you hydrated. When you're out in the sun all day, it's important to make sure you're getting enough fluids. And what better way to do that than by eating delicious fruit?

I prefer to shop for fruits by season, but some fruits are great year-round. Typically, fruits that perform best at picnics are small, easy to pick up, and mess-free. These fruits are all relatively small and easy to eat, and they're also packed with flavor. Berries in particular are a great choice for picnics because they're already bite-sized. Grapes and cherries are also good options, as they can be eaten without needing to be cut up. Figs and apricots are slightly harder to eat but are still delicious, and peaches are a classic picnic fruit that always goes down well.

Appetizers

Bruschetta

The sun was shining brightly, and the warm breeze rustled through the trees. The smell of freshly chopped herbs wafted through the air making it almost feel like summer already. It was a perfect day for a picnic.

Bruschetta is a delicious Italian appetizer that can be made in just a few minutes. Perfect for a starter or appetizer.

Ingredients:
This will make enough bruschetta for an appetizer for 4 to 6.
1 loaf crusty bread (I prefer sourdough)
¼ cup olive oil (60 ml)
4 garlic cloves
6 ounces cherry tomatoes (170 g)
¼ cup basil, chopped (5 g)
salt and pepper, to taste
flaky salt to top

Steps:

Step 1: Cut the bread lengthwise and toast until it is crispy.

Step 2: Cut 1 of the garlic cloves and rub it over each of the slices of bread.

Step 3: Cut the cherry tomatoes, chop the basil leaves, and mince the other 3 garlic cloves. Combine in a bowl and gently toss. Add salt and pepper to taste.

Step 4: Spoon the tomato mixture over the garlic bread slices.

Step 5: Garnish with fresh basil leaves and flaky salt. Enjoy!

Melon Prosciutto Skewers

Melon prosciutto skewers are made by combining two delightful ingredients: ripe, sweet melon and salty prosciutto. The melon provides a succulent and juicy contrast to the savory ham, while the skewer helps to keep everything neatly in place. If you're entertaining a large picnic party, these skewers are perfect.

Ingredients:
This will make 8 skewers.
½ small cantaloupe or honeydew melon, cut into bite-sized cubes
4 slices prosciutto, cut in half lengthwise
8 small fresh basil leaves
6–8 mini mozzarella balls
8 skewers (if using wooden skewers, soak in water for 30 minutes before using)
balsamic vinegar and olive oil

Steps:

Step 1: Cut your melon open and use a melon baller.

Step 2: To make your own melon prosciutto skewers, simply thread chunks of cantaloupe or honeydew onto wooden skewers, alternating with thin slices of prosciutto di Parma. If you're feeling fancy, you can also add a piece of fresh mozzarella or a small basil leaf to each skewer.

Step 3: Drizzle with balsamic vinegar and olive oil. Once assembled, the skewers can be transported easily (just be sure to bring them back to room temperature before serving). Enjoy!

Croquettes

As I begin to gather my ingredients, a sense of calm settles over me. The floury texture feels comforting against my skin. As I knead and shape the dough, I find myself slipping into a sense of peacefulness.

Croquettes are an iconic dish consisting of a fried patty of mashed potatoes and other ingredients. Usually, they are then coated in fine bread crumbs before being fried to perfection. Variations on the classic include components such as beef, seafood and vegetable.

Ingredients:
This will make 6–8 large croquettes.
1 pound of potatoes (450 g)
1 egg
¼ cup of panko or breadcrumbs (60 ml)
¼ cup of grated Parmesan cheese (optional) (60 ml or about 25 g for Parmesan)
1–2 tablespoons of finely chopped fresh herbs (optional) (15–30 ml)
1 teaspoon of salt (5 ml)
½ teaspoon of pepper (2.5 ml)
1 tablespoon of vegetable oil (15 ml)

Steps:

Step 1: Preheat your air fryer to 400°F or 205°C.

Step 2: Peel and cut the potatoes into small pieces and place in a pot. Boil for 10 minutes, or until they are soft. Drain and mash with a fork or potato masher.

Step 3: In a bowl, whisk together the egg, bread crumbs, salt, and pepper. If using, add the grated cheese and chopped herbs to the mixture. Add this mixture to the potatoes and stir until everything is evenly mixed.

Step 4: Shape the potato mixture into small patties and then coat in the vegetable oil.

Step 5: Place the croquettes in the air fryer and cook for 15 minutes, or until they are golden brown and crispy. Serve immediately with your favorite dipping sauce.

Fresh Spring Rolls

Fresh spring rolls or summer rolls are a type of Vietnamese wrap that is perfect for a light meal or snack. The wraps are made from rice paper, which is filled with a variety of ingredients including rice noodles, meat, vegetables, and herbs. The wraps are then rolled up and served with a dipping sauce. Fresh spring rolls are extremely refreshing and can be customized to suit any taste.

Ingredients:
This will make 8 spring rolls.
8 rice paper rounds
2 ounces rice noodles (57 g)
1 cup shredded purple cabbage (about 70 g)
½ cup shredded carrot (about 60 g)
½ cup thinly sliced cucumber (about 60 g)
8–10 fresh basil leaves
4 ounces protein of choice (such as cooked shrimp, sliced chicken, or tofu) (113 g)

Peanut sauce:
1 tablespoon minced garlic (15 ml)
1 cup peanut butter (240 ml or about 270 g for smooth peanut butter)
2 tablespoons hoisin sauce (30 ml)
½ cup water (120 ml)
½ tablespoon brown sugar (about 7 g)
a drizzle of oil

Steps:

Step 1: Prepare your vegetables. Thinly slice the cabbage, carrot, cucumber, and basil.

Step 2: Soak the rice noodles until softened, following the noodle packaging instructions.

Step 3: Then, assemble the rolls. Wet a piece of rice paper with water. Do not over-soak. Lay the vegetables and shrimp neatly in the middle of the rice paper.

Step 4: Fold the bottom corner up over the filling, then fold in the sides. Roll up tightly to enclose the filling. Repeat with the remaining spring roll wrappers and filling.

Step 5: Wrap each spring roll individually in plastic wrap to prevent sticking. Serve the same day, or immediately, as they do not keep well in the fridge. If storing in the fridge, wrap tightly with plastic wrap when wet and store in an airtight container to prevent drying out.

Step 6: To make the peanut sauce, add oil and garlic in a saucepan on medium low heat. Gently heat for about 30 seconds. Add the peanut butter with hoisin sauce. Stir until combined and then add water. Add brown sugar and reduce. Optional: add chili sauce with the peanut sauce.

Tip: You can customize your peanut sauce!

- Add a sour component: Adding a bit of lime juice or vinegar can bring a fresh, tangy note to your peanut sauce, balancing the richness of the peanut butter.
- Add some heat: Adding some chili sauce or a pinch of red pepper flakes can give the sauce a nice kick.
- Soy sauce: A splash of soy sauce can add some depth and umami flavor.
- Adjust the sweetener: If you find the sauce too sweet or not sweet enough, you can adjust the amount of brown sugar to your liking.

Fried Chicken Bites

Chicken karaage is a popular Japanese dish that is served as an appetizer or main course. The dish features bite-sized pieces of chicken that are marinated, coated with potato starch, and deep-fried until golden brown. The result is juicy and tender chicken with a crispy, flavorful coating.

Ingredients:
This will make enough for a main course for 2 or appetizer for 4-6.
1 pound boneless, skinless chicken thighs (450 g)
¼ cup soy sauce (60 ml)
¼ cup sake (Japanese rice wine) (60 ml)
2 tablespoons grated ginger (30 ml)
2 cloves garlic, minced
1 tablespoon sesame oil (15 ml)
½ cup all-purpose flour (about 60 g)
½ cup potato starch (about 60 g)
oil for frying
salt and pepper to taste

Steps:

Step 1: Cut the chicken thighs into bite-sized pieces and set aside.

Step 2: In a large bowl, mix together the soy sauce, sake, grated ginger, minced garlic, and sesame oil. Add the chicken to the marinade, making sure each piece is coated. Cover the bowl and refrigerate for at least one hour, or up to overnight.

Step 3: In a shallow dish, mix together the flour, potato starch, salt, and pepper.

Step 4: Heat oil in a deep fryer or large pot until it reaches 350°F (175°C).

Step 5: Remove the chicken from the marinade and allow any excess to drip off.

Step 6: Coat each piece of chicken in the flour mixture, shaking off any excess.

Step 7: Carefully add the coated chicken to the hot oil, frying in batches if necessary. Fry for about 4 to 5 minutes, or until the chicken is golden brown and cooked through.

Step 8: Use a slotted spoon to remove the chicken from the oil, placing it onto a paper towel-lined plate to drain off any excess oil.

Step 9: Serve the chicken karaage hot, garnished with thinly sliced green onions and a sprinkle of sesame seeds.

Miso Chicken Skewers

Skewers provide hosts with an effortless way to feed guests, sparing them the hassle and mess that comes with typical party food. They look lovely when presented together on trays, too. There's no need for knives or forks—just pick them up and eat!

Deliciously aromatic, this simple chicken skewer recipe is sure to become one of your go-to dishes for any gathering. Marinating the bite-sized pieces of chicken in miso gives it a complex layer of flavor that will leave everyone wanting more.

Ingredients:
This makes enough for 2 for an appetizer.
2 boneless, skinless chicken thighs (cut into cubes)
2 tablespoons miso paste (30 ml)
2 tablespoons honey (30 ml)
1 tablespoon soy sauce (15 ml)
1 tablespoon rice vinegar (15 ml)
3 garlic cloves (minced)
1 tablespoon sesame oil (15 ml)
½ tablespoon white cooking wine (7.5 ml)
1 teaspoon grated fresh ginger (5 ml)
salt and pepper to taste
4 wooden skewers (soaked in water for at least 30 minutes)

Steps:

Step 1: In a bowl, mix the miso paste, honey, soy sauce, rice vinegar, garlic, sesame oil, ginger, salt, and pepper together until it forms a thick marinade.

Step 2: Add the chicken cubes to the bowl and mix until the chicken is completely coated with the marinade. Cover the bowl with plastic wrap and refrigerate for at least 2 hours, or overnight to allow the flavors to develop.

Step 3: Take out the chicken from the fridge and let sit at room temperature for 10 to 15 minutes.

Step 4: Thread the chicken cubes onto the wooden skewers, leaving some space between cubes.

Step 5: Preheat your grill to medium-high heat, around 375–400°F (190–205°C). Grill the skewers for 10 to 15 minutes, turning them over occasionally, until the chicken is fully cooked through and has a nice char on the outside.

Step 6: Once the chicken is done, remove the skewers from the grill and let them rest for a few minutes before serving.

Step 7: Serve the miso chicken skewers warm, garnished with chopped scallions and a sprinkle of sesame seeds.

Glazed Tteokbokki Skewers

Tteokbokki is a beloved Korean dish of chewy rice cakes smothered in a fiery and sweet red sauce. It's usually accompanied by a medley of vegetables and protein such as fish cakes, boiled eggs, and onions. Tteokboki recipes can vary from region to region and even household to household, with some opting for a milder sauce.

Ingredients:
This will make 4 medium length skewers.
1 cup sliced Korean rice cakes (about 150 g)
8–12 small size wieners (same length as the rice cakes)
¼ cup chopped green onion (roughly 25 g)
2 tablespoons vegetable oil (30 ml)
4 wooden skewers
For the glaze:
2 tablespoons soy sauce (30 ml)
2 tablespoons honey (30 ml)
2 cloves garlic, minced
1 tablespoon gochujang (Korean chili paste) (15 ml)
1 tablespoon rice vinegar (15 ml)
1 tablespoon sesame oil (15 ml)
1 tablespoon sesame seeds (about 9 g)
2 tablespoons water (30 ml)

Steps:

Step 1: Soak the wooden skewers in water for at least 30 minutes to prevent burning.

Step 2: Thread the rice cakes and sausages, alternating, onto the skewers.

Step 3: Heat the vegetable oil in a nonstick pan over medium-high heat. Add the skewers and cook for 2 to 3 minutes on each side or until lightly browned.

Step 4: In the meantime, prepare the glaze by combining all the glaze ingredients in a small saucepan. Heat over medium heat, stirring frequently, until the mixture thickens and the flavors are well combined.

Step 5: Brush the glaze over the skewers, making sure to coat them evenly.

Step 6: Serve the glazed tteokbokki skewers hot, garnished with chopped green onions and additional sesame seeds for extra texture and flavor.

Spicy Shrimp Kebabs

Aromatic spices fill the air. Summer is the time to fire up the grill and enjoy some savory flavors while basking in the sun. There is nothing better than enjoying seafood while grilling in the company of your loved ones. These spicy shrimp kebabs are easy to eat and a crowd pleaser. Customize this recipe with additional vegetables or keep it simple. Either way, this is an unforgettable summer treat.

Ingredients:

This will make 4–6 skewers.

½ lb. large shrimp, peeled and deveined (225 g)
2 tablespoons olive oil (30 ml)
3 cloves garlic, minced
1 teaspoon cumin (5 ml)
1 teaspoon smoked paprika (5 ml)
½ teaspoon cayenne pepper (2.5 ml)
salt and pepper, to taste
1 lemon cut into wedges for garnish
4–6 wooden skewers, soaked in water

Steps:

Step 1: If you're using a grill, preheat it to medium-high heat. If you're using a stove, preheat your grill pan over medium-high heat.

Step 2: Evenly thread shrimp onto skewers (about 2 to 3 shrimp per skewer, depending on the size).

Step 3: In a small bowl, whisk together olive oil, garlic, cumin, smoked paprika, cayenne pepper, and salt and pepper for the marinade.

Step 4: Brush the spice mixture generously over the shrimp, making sure they are all coated evenly.

Step 5: Grill the skewers for 2 to 3 minutes per side or until the shrimp turn pink and cooked through. Remember that shrimp cooks quickly, so be sure to monitor it closely to prevent it from becoming rubbery.

Step 6: Serve with a squeeze of lemon.

Pork and Green Onion Pan-Fried Dumplings

I was fascinated by the precision and care with which my mother assembled the dumplings. Each plump and perfectly formed dumpling was a testament to her skill and dedication to perfection. The aroma of the succulent pork and fragrant green onions mingling together was enough to make my mouth water and my heart skip a beat.

As we worked together, my mother would share the secrets and techniques passed down through generations of her family. She would demonstrate the deft hand movements needed to crimp each dumpling perfectly.

Ingredients:
This will make approximately 15–20 dumplings.
½ cup ground pork (about 115 g)
¼ cup finely chopped green onions (about 25 g)
2 cloves minced garlic
2 tablespoons minced ginger (30 ml)
½ tablespoon soy sauce (7.5 ml)
½ teaspoon sesame oil (2.5 ml)
½ teaspoon salt (2.5 ml)
¼ teaspoon sugar (roughly 1.25 ml or 1 g)
¼ teaspoon white pepper (about 1.25 ml)
2 tablespoons vegetable oil (30 ml)
sesame seeds and chopped green onion for garnish
For the dipping sauce:
1 tablespoon black vinegar (15 ml)
1 tablespoon chili oil (15 ml)
1 tablespoon soy sauce (15 ml)
small pinch of sugar

Steps:

Step 1: In a large mixing bowl, combine the ground pork, finely chopped green onions, minced garlic, soy sauce, sesame oil, salt, sugar, and pepper. Mix everything together until well combined.

Step 2: Place a dumpling wrapper on a flat surface and spoon 1 tablespoon of the pork filling into the center of the wrapper.

Step 3: Using your fingers, wet the edges of the wrapper with water and fold it in half, pressing the edges to create a crimp to seal the dumpling. Repeat until all of the filling has been used.

Step 4: In a large skillet, heat 2 tablespoons of vegetable oil over medium-high heat. Once the oil is hot, add the dumplings to the skillet in a single layer, flat side down.

Step 5: Cook the dumplings for 2 to 3 minutes or until they are golden brown on one side.

Step 6: Add ½ cup of water to the skillet and cover it with a tight-fitting lid. Let the dumplings steam for 5 to 7 minutes or until the water has evaporated.

Step 7: Remove the lid and continue to cook the dumplings for another minute or two until they are crispy and golden brown.

Step 8: Serve hot with your favorite dipping sauce. Add sesame seeds and additional green onion for garnish.

Tips on Dumpling Making:

When it comes to wrapping the dumplings, there are a few important tips to keep in mind.

- Make sure to use a generous amount of filling, but do not overfill the dumpling as this can cause the wrapper to break or tear during cooking.
- Pleats can be added by folding the edges of the wrapper and pressing them together to create a beautiful, decorative finish.
- It is vital to keep the wrappers unopened until you're ready to use them. The packaging is designed to protect the wrappers from air and moisture, which can quickly dry them out and make them brittle.
- Store unused dumpling wrappers in the fridge in an airtight container. If you need to store for a longer period, the freezer is the best option. Freezing the wrappers in an airtight container keeps them fresh for up to several months.

Pork and Chive Baos

Pork and chive pan-fried baos are a popular and delicious Chinese dish that you can make at home with a few simple ingredients. The key to making the perfect baos is the dough, which should be soft and fluffy with a golden brown crust on the bottom.

This savory snack is filled with pork and soup broth, and perfectly cooked to bring out the mouthwatering flavor of the ingredients. But there's one crucial step in enjoying this treat that shouldn't be overlooked—eating it as soon as you can! This might be counterintuitive for a picnic, but I assure you that these are portable, delicious, and a nice change from typical picnic fare.

Ingredients:
Makes six to eight large baos.
6 ounces ground pork (170 g)
6–8 pieces bao dough (can be store-bought or homemade)
¼ cup chopped chives (about 25 g)
¼ cup chopped green onion (about 25 g)
1 tablespoon soy sauce (15 ml)
1 tablespoon sesame oil (15 ml)
1 tablespoon Shaoxing wine (15 ml)
1 tablespoon grated ginger (15 ml)
1 teaspoon sugar (about 4 g)
1 teaspoon salt (5 ml)
¼ teaspoon white pepper (about 1.25 ml)
1 tablespoon vegetable oil (15 ml)
¼ cup water (60 ml)
For the bao dough:
1 cup all-purpose flour (about 125 g)
½ teaspoon active dry yeast (about 1.5 g)
½ teaspoon sugar (roughly 2.5 ml or 2 g)
¼ to ½ cup lukewarm water (60 ml to 120 ml)

Steps:

To make the bao dough:

Step 1: In a small mixing bowl, add the active dry yeast and sugar to the lukewarm water. Stir thoroughly until the yeast and sugar are completely dissolved. Then, set the bowl aside and wait for the mixture to become frothy, which should take approximately 5 to 10 minutes.

Step 2: In a separate mixing bowl, add the all-purpose flour and make a well in the center. Pour the frothy yeast mixture into the well and start mixing with a spoon until the ingredients are combined.

Step 3: Once the ingredients are combined, start kneading the dough with your hands for about 5 to 10 minutes until it becomes smooth and elastic.

Step 4: Once the dough is smooth and elastic, cover the mixing bowl with a damp cloth and let the dough rest for about 1 hour in a warm and humid place. This will help it to rise and become fluffy.

Step 5: After the dough has rested for an hour, take it out of the mixing bowl and start forming it into a round shape. Then, divide the dough into four equal pieces.

To make the baos:

Step 1: In a large mixing bowl, combine the ground pork, chopped chives, soy sauce, sesame oil, Shaoxing wine, grated ginger, sugar, salt, and white pepper. Mix well, using a fork or your hands, until all the ingredients are evenly distributed.

Step 2: Take one piece of bao dough and roll it into a flat disc with a thickness of about 3 mm. Spoon a quarter of the pork and chive filling onto the center of the disc, then pleat and pinch the edges of the dough together to seal the filling inside. Repeat with the remaining dough and filling to make a total of four baos.

Step 3: Heat up a flat-bottomed pan over medium heat and add 1 tablespoon of vegetable oil. Once the oil is hot, place the baos into the pan with the pleated side facing up. Let the baos fry for about 2 to 3 minutes, or until the bottom is golden brown and crispy.

Step 4: Pour ¼ cup of water into the pan and immediately cover it with a lid. Let the baos steam for about 5 minutes, or until the water has evaporated and the dough is cooked through.

Step 5: Remove the lid and continue frying the baos for another 1 to 2 minutes, or until the bottom is extra crispy and caramelized. Use a spatula to carefully remove the baos from the pan and transfer them to a serving plate.

Step 6: Serve the pork and chive pan-fried baos hot, with a side of black vinegar and ginger sauce or chili oil for dipping.

Side Dishes

Grilled Vegetables

Grilled vegetables are a delightful way to start any picnic. Choose from heartier root vegetables like onions and parsnips or sweeter options like peppers or spiced corn on the cob. Softened and lightly charred, each vegetable carries a distinct flavor. They are also extremely low maintenance! If you do not desire to grill at your destination, you can prepare the vegetables ahead of time to enjoy.

Ingredients:
This will make 8 skewers.
1 small zucchini, sliced into quarter-inch rounds
1 small yellow squash, sliced into quarter-inch rounds
1 small red onion, cut into wedges
1 small red bell pepper, seeded and cut into bite-sized pieces
1 small yellow bell pepper, seeded and cut into bite-sized pieces
1 small orange bell pepper, seeded and cut into bite-sized pieces
2 tablespoons olive oil (30 ml)
1 tablespoon balsamic vinegar (15 ml)
1 teaspoon dried oregano (5 ml)
½ teaspoon garlic powder (2.5 ml)
salt and pepper to taste
8 skewers (if using wooden skewers, soak in water for 30 minutes before using)

Steps:

Step 1: Preheat your grill to medium-high heat. If you are using a pan, let the pan heat up until sizzling hot.

Step 2: Soak your wooden skewers.

Step 3: In a small bowl, combine the olive oil, balsamic vinegar, dried oregano, garlic powder, salt, and pepper. Set aside.

Step 4: Thread the vegetables in alternating colors. Start with a larger piece at the bottom and work your way up, alternating between bell peppers, onion, squash, and zucchini.

Step 5: Coat your skewers in the olive oil mixture.

Step 6: Cook the skewers on the grill or on a hot pan for 8 to 10 minutes or until slightly charred. You can keep the skewers as they make for easy eating on your picnic.

Step 7: Set aside to cool and pack in a long container.

Enoki Mushroom Beef Rolls

Enoki mushrooms are a type of fungi that have been enjoyed in Asian cuisine for centuries. These delicate mushrooms are commonly used in salads, soups, hotpots, and stir-fries. Their slender, white stalks and tiny golden caps make them a visually appealing addition to any dish.

Ingredients:

½ pound thinly sliced beef (about 225 g)
1 package enoki mushrooms
2 cloves garlic, minced
2 tablespoons soy sauce (30 ml)
1 tablespoon sugar (roughly 12 g)
1 tablespoon black pepper (roughly 12 g)
1 teaspoon sesame oil (5 ml)
toothpicks

Steps:

Step 1: Prepare the enoki mushrooms. Trim the bottoms to remove any dirt or debris.

Step 2: In a small bowl, mix together the minced garlic, soy sauce, sugar, black pepper, and sesame oil..

Step 3: Place a slice of beef on a clean cutting board. Place enoki and roll tightly, securing with a toothpick. Repeat.

Step 4: Heat a nonstick pan over medium-high heat. Add the beef rolls and cook until browned, about 2 to 3 minutes per side.

Step 5: Brush the garlic soy sauce glaze onto the rolls and let cook for an additional 1 or 2 minutes until the sauce has thickened and the beef is cooked through.

Fried Tempura

Fried tempura is a widely popular Japanese delicacy that has gained immense popularity. A perfect blend of crispiness and lightness, this dish is a true delight for everyone. The thought of preparing this dish at home might seem daunting and intimidating, but it is much easier than it appears. All you need is your favorite vegetables or protein and the right technique, and you'll have a plate of perfectly crunchy and tasty tempura in no time.

Ingredients:
This will make enough for 3–4 people.

10–12 pieces of your favorite seasonal, assorted vegetables (such as sweet potato, eggplant, lotus root, broccoli, shishito peppers, shiso), cut into bite-sized pieces
6–10 raw shrimp, peeled and deveined
1 cup all-purpose flour (about 125 g)
½ cup cornstarch (about 60 g)
1 cup sparkling water (240 ml)
½ teaspoon salt (about 3 g)
¼ teaspoon black pepper (about 0.5 g)
vegetable oil for frying

Tempura Frying Tips:

- Add a little cornstarch to tempura batter for a crispy texture. It prevents the batter from becoming thick or doughy and reduces oil absorption.
- For crispy tempura, fry at 350–375°F (176–191°C). This temperature quickly forms a delicious light crust. If the oil is too hot, the tempura may become too brown and overcooked, while if the oil is too cold, the batter may absorb too much oil and turn soggy.
- Soda water in tempura batter creates bubbles, resulting in a lighter and crispier texture.
- Use cold water to prevent excess gluten formation in tempura batter. This keeps the batter light and thin, avoiding a heavy, dense texture.

Preparing the Shrimp:

Shrimp tempura is a popular dish in many parts of the world, known for its crispy texture and delicate flavor. However, preparing the shrimp for tempura can be a challenging task, especially if you want to achieve a flat and even shape. Here is a step-by-step tutorial to guide you on how to prepare shrimp for tempura.

Step 1: Shell removal and deveining

Remove the head and shell, leaving the tail. Slit the back and gently remove the vein.

Step 2: Butterflying the shrimp

Turn shrimp over and make shallow cuts along the length. Spread open and press down to flatten. This prevents the shrimp from curling when fried.

Step 3: Dry the shrimp thoroughly and trim the tail

Dry the shrimp thoroughly before frying in tempura batter to make sure that the hot oil does not splash. Blot shrimp with a paper towel until dry. Trim the tail to a V-shape and squeeze out any excess water.

Now your shrimps are ready to be battered!

Steps:

Step 1: In a large bowl, sift together the flour, cornstarch, salt, and black pepper until combined.

Step 2: Slowly pour the cold sparkling water into the bowl while whisking to create a smooth batter. You can also use regular cold water, but sparkling water creates a fluffier texture. Add the vegetables and shrimp to the tempura batter and mix until evenly coated.

Step 3: Place a medium-sized pot over medium-high heat and add enough vegetable oil to reach a depth of two inches. Heat the oil until it reaches 350°F (175°C).

Step 4: Using a pair of tongs, carefully place the coated vegetables and shrimp into the hot oil. Fry until they are golden brown and crispy, about 3 to 4 minutes. Be sure to turn the pieces occasionally to ensure even cooking. If using an air fryer instead of a deep fryer, replace the vegetable oil with cooking spray and preheat the air fryer to 400°F. Fry for 10–15 minutes until golden and crispy.

Step 5: Once done, place the tempura on a paper towel-lined plate or rack to remove excess oil. Season with salt to taste.

Step 6: Package the tempura for your picnic. Use parchment paper underneath the tempura to blot the excess oil while in transport. It is important to wait until the tempura is completely cool before packing or it will become soggy.

Tonkatsu

As I entered the traditional restaurant, the aroma of tonkatsu filled the air, igniting my senses and sending my taste buds into overdrive. The ambience was enchanting, with soft lighting and a distinctly rustic feel that transported me to another time and place. I glanced out the window as I awaited my order. And then it came. Breaded pork with a side of cabbage salad and warm rice. My first bite was pure bliss—the outer layer of the tonkatsu was crispy and savory, while the interior was incredibly tender and juicy. The accompanying dipping sauce added just the right amount of tanginess to the dish, creating a harmonic flavor profile that left me wanting more. Suddenly I felt a warmth wash over me.

Ingredients:

This will make 2 portions.

2 boneless pork chops (about a half-inch thick)
1 cup panko breadcrumbs (about 60 g)
¼ cup all-purpose flour (about 30 g)
1 egg
vegetable oil for frying

For the sauce:

2 tablespoons ketchup (30 ml)
1 tablespoon Worcestershire sauce (15 ml)
1 tablespoon soy sauce (15 ml)
1 teaspoon sugar (about 4 g)

Steps:

To make the tonkatsu:

Step 1: Start by preparing the pork chops. Take a meat mallet and pound the pork chops until they are about a quarter-inch thick. Season them with salt and pepper on both sides.

Step 2: Set up a breading station. In three bowls, separate the flour, beaten egg, and panko breadcrumbs.

Step 3: Dredge the pork chops in the flour, shaking off any excess. Then, dip them in the egg mixture and coat them with the panko breadcrumbs.

Step 4: Heat about half an inch of oil in a large skillet over medium-high heat. Once the oil is hot, gently place the pork chops in the skillet and cook them for 3 to 4 minutes on each side or until they are golden brown and crispy and katsu is cooked through.

Alternate: If you would like to use an air fryer, you can also air fry at 390°F (200°C) for 12 to 15 minutes flipping once.

Step 5 Drain the tonkatsu on a sheet of paper towel or rack to remove any excess oil.

Step 6: Slice the tonkatsu into strips so that it is easy to eat. Let the tonkatsu cool completely before packing away to ensure it stays crisp!

To make the katsu sauce:

Step 1: Mix together the ketchup, Worcestershire sauce, soy sauce, and sugar in a small bowl. You can also buy premade tonkatsu sauce.

To serve:

- Slice the tonkatsu into strips so that it is easy to eat. Let the tonkatsu cool completely before packing away to ensure it stays crisp!
- Pack the tonkatsu with parchment paper so that any excess oil is absorbed. Serve the tonkatsu with a side of the cabbage salad and tonkatsu sauce.

Salads

Fruit Salad

A fruit salad is a beautiful thing. It captures the colors and bounty of the season. As I slice through a juicy pear, I can't help but think of the sweetness of spring.

For those who wish to prepare a delectable fruit salad in a matter of minutes, all that's necessary is an assortment of your favorite fruits. A bit of mint or cinnamon can enhance the flavors further and, to top it off, you could toss the mixture with a bit of honey or maple syrup for a hint of sweetness. With this simple ingredient list, you can create an exquisite fruit salad in no time at all.

Ingredients:

This will make enough for 2–4 people.
Feel free to substitute with your favorite fruits.
1 cup strawberries, hulled and halved (about 150 g)
½ cup raspberries (65 g)
½ cup blueberries (75 g)
1 kiwi, peeled and sliced (100 g)
½ cup grapes (75 g)
2 tablespoons honey (42 g)
4 sprigs of fresh mint
splash of lemon juice or orange juice

Steps:

Step 1: Cut the fruit into bite-sized pieces and place in a large bowl.

Step 2: Add a splash of orange juice or lemon juice to add sweetness and prevent the fruit from browning.

Step 3: Gently stir the ingredients together until evenly mixed.

Step 4: Top the fruit mixture with a hint of honey or brown sugar. Add freshly cut mint to top.

Peach Burrata Salad

As the sun blazes and the heat of the summer season sets in, I can't help but crave a light and refreshing salad that truly captures the essence of the season. And for me, nothing quite matches the freshness and indulgence of a burrata salad. This dish is perfect for summertime gatherings—it's light, refreshing, and full of flavor.

Ingredients:
This will make enough for 2–4 people.
1 large peach, sliced (about 150 g to 175 g)
4 ounces of burrata cheese or a large ball (about 113 g)
½ cup cherry tomato (optional, about 75 g to 85 g)
five sprigs of basil
1 tablespoon balsamic vinegar (about 15 ml)
1 tablespoon olive oil (about 15 ml)
salt and pepper to taste

Steps:

Step 1: Start by slicing the peaches into thin wedges. Slice the cherry tomatoes in half. Tear the burrata into bite-sized pieces.

Step 2: Add the peaches, tomatoes, and burrata into your dish, along with some chopped basil leaves.

Step 3: Drizzle with olive oil and balsamic vinegar, season with salt and pepper to taste.

Step 4: Serve with warm toasted bread on the side to turn this dish into an appetizer.

Yuzu Cabbage Salad

Yuzu is a citrus fruit and is highly versatile. The zest and juice are often used in marinades, dressings, and sauces but can also be commonly found in cocktails and desserts.

While fresh yuzu can be difficult to find, premade yuzu juice is widely available and can be found at specialty stores. Alternatively, if you are unable to find yuzu, you can substitute it with lemon juice, which will provide a similar tartness and acidic quality.

Ingredients:
This will make enough for 2-4 people.
2 cups shredded green cabbage (about 150 g to 200 g)
2 tablespoons freshly squeezed yuzu juice (or substitute with lemon or lime juice) (about 30 ml)
1 tablespoon rice vinegar (about 15 ml)
1 teaspoon soy sauce (about 5 ml)
1 teaspoon honey (7 g)
¼ teaspoon grated ginger (about 1 g)
1 tablespoon vegetable oil (about 15 ml)
pinch of salt

Steps:

Step 1: Thinly slice your cabbage. Cutting cabbage thinly for salads is a simple process that can be done quickly and easily with the right tools. Cut off the bottom of the cabbage to create a flat base for stability. Using a sharp knife, slice the cabbage into thin discs or thin strips. For an even thinner result, use a mandolin slicer on the thinnest setting.

Step 2: In a medium-sized bowl, whisk together the yuzu juice, rice vinegar, soy sauce, honey, grated ginger, salt, and vegetable oil until well combined.

Step 3: Add the shredded green cabbage to the bowl and toss until the cabbage is fully coated with the dressing.

Step 4: Let the cabbage marinate in the dressing for at least 10 minutes to allow the flavors to meld together.

Simple Tangy Potato Salad

A simple potato salad that is refreshing and easy to make for even the most beginner of picnic chefs. This recipe comes together quickly and easily with just the right ingredients. Perfect as a side or main for summer picnics, pool parties, or potlucks, this refreshingly delectable salad captures all the comforting flavors of classic potato salads while adding its own unique zesty twist.

Ingredients:
This will make enough for 2–4 people.
4 small red potatoes (about 450 g)
2 tablespoons diced red onion (30 g)
2 tablespoons chopped fresh dill (8 g)
1 tablespoon Dijon mustard (15 ml)
1 tablespoon whole-grain mustard (15 ml)
1 tablespoon apple cider vinegar (15 ml)
2 tablespoons extra-virgin olive oil (30 ml)
salt and pepper, to taste

Steps:

Step 1: Begin by washing the potatoes; peel if desired. Cut them into bite-sized pieces that are roughly the same size. Boil the potatoes in salted water until they're tender, which should take around 10 to 12 minutes. Once they're cooked, drain them and let them cool completely.

Step 2: While the potatoes are boiling, chop up the red onion and dill. Set them aside in a medium mixing bowl.

Step 3: In a small mixing bowl, whisk together the Dijon mustard, whole-grain mustard, apple cider vinegar, and extra-virgin olive oil. Add salt and pepper to taste.

Step 4: Once the potatoes have cooled, add them to the bowl with the red onion and dill. Pour the mustard dressing over the top and toss everything together. Taste your potato salad and adjust any seasoning if necessary.

Step 5: Serve immediately or store in an airtight container until you're ready to eat it. This potato salad will keep well at room temperature for several hours.

Some additional tips to make your potato salad even tastier:

- Use fresh herbs, such as dill or parsley, to give your salad a burst of flavor.
- Try choosing a different type of mustard to make your dressing. Spicy brown or honey mustard could also work well!
- For an extra tangy kick, add some chopped pickles or pickled vegetables to your salad.
- If you're not a fan of red onions, try using diced shallots or scallions instead.

Roasted Root Vegetable Salad

A root vegetable salad is such a versatile dish—able to bring out the best in any assortment of vegetables. Its crunchy texture and versatility of flavors can either add vibrant flair to an appetizer spread or turn into a wholesome side dish. Each bite of this hearty dish bursts with flavor and succulent texture. The best part is that this salad can be made ahead of time and stored!

Ingredients:
This will make 4-6 servings.
2 large potatoes or sweet potatoes (about 500 g)
2 large carrots (about 300 g to 350 g)
4-5 beets (about 450 g to 600 g)
3 tablespoons fresh parsley (about 15 g)
2 ounces goat cheese (56 g)
8 ounces arugula (227 g)
Dressing:
¼ cup olive oil (60 ml)
salt
pepper
2 tablespoon champagne vinegar (30 ml)
1 tablespoon horseradish (15 ml)
1 tablespoon Dijon mustard (15 ml)
fresh fennel

Steps:

Step 1: Preheat the oven to 425°F (220°C)

Step 2: Start by peeling and chopping your root vegetables.

Step 3: Line a pan with parchment paper. Toss root vegetables with a generous amount of olive oil and salt and pepper. Spread on a baking sheet and roast for 35 to 40 minutes, stirring once or twice, until tender and lightly browned.

Step 4: While the vegetables are roasting, prepare the vinaigrette. In a small bowl, whisk together the olive oil, champagne vinegar, horseradish, Dijon mustard, and a pinch of salt and pepper. Stir in the sliced fennel.

Step 5: In a large bowl, combine roasted vegetables, arugula, goat cheese, and vinaigrette. Serve warm or cold.

Rice Noodle Salad

This rice noodle salad is a wonderful mix of flavors and textures, from the tender noodles to the crunchy vegetables and the nutty peanuts. The sesame oil and soy sauce dressing adds depth and richness to the dish, while the lime juice and honey balance the flavors with a tangy and sweet kick. You can also experiment with different ingredients, such as adding cooked shrimp, shredded chicken, or tofu for extra protein.

Ingredients:
This will make 4–6 servings.
8 ounces rice noodles (227 g)
1 carrot, shredded (75 g)
1 cucumber, cut into thin matchsticks (150 g)
1 red bell pepper, sliced (150 g)
3 scallions, sliced (45 g)
¼ cup cilantro, chopped (15 g)
¼ cup peanuts, chopped (about 35 g)
1 tablespoon red pepper flakes (5 g)
1 tablespoon sesame oil (15 ml)
2 tablespoons soy sauce (30 ml)
1 tablespoon honey (15 ml)
juice of 1 lime (about 30 ml)
salt and pepper to taste

Steps:

Step 1: Bring a large pot of water to a rolling boil. Add the rice noodles and cook for 3 to 4 minutes or until tender. Drain and rinse under cold water.

Step 2: In a large bowl, whisk together the sesame oil, soy sauce, honey, lime juice, and red pepper flakes. Add salt and pepper to taste.

Step 3: Add the cooked rice noodles, shredded carrot, cucumber, red bell pepper, scallions and cilantro to the bowl with the dressing. Toss well to combine and top with chopped peanuts

Tip: To prevent the noodles from sticking, add sesame oil before the vinaigrette. Rice noodles can be prone to clumping but the oil will help.

Fresh Lotus Root Salad

Lotus root has been a part of my life ever since I was a small child. I can remember standing on tippy toes at the stovetop watching my mother cook. She would make the most delicious soups and stir-fries.

Every time I prepare this dish, I remember the smell of spices gently wafting through the kitchen; laughter mixing with conversation over dinner; warmth radiating around us. These memories serve as a reminder of how powerful food can be for creating connections between people and connecting us all.

Ingredients:
This will make 2–3 servings.
1 lotus root, peeled and sliced into thin rounds (about 200 g)
2 cups water (480 ml)
1 teaspoon salt (5 g)
2 tablespoons rice vinegar (30 ml)
1 green onion, thinly sliced (15 g)
1 tablespoon toasted sesame seeds (10 g)
1 tablespoon sesame oil (15 ml)
1 teaspoon soy sauce (5 ml)
1 teaspoon honey (7 g)
1 teaspoon ginger, minced (5 g)
1 clove garlic, minced (5 g)
¼ teaspoon red pepper flakes (1.5 g)

Steps:

Step 1: Rinse the lotus root thoroughly under cold water. Then peel and slice into thin rounds.

Step 2: In a pot, bring water to a boil and add ½ tsp of salt. Add the sliced lotus root and cook for 7 to 10 minutes until tender but still crispy. Drain and rinse with cold water.

Step 3: In a mixing bowl, toss the cooked lotus root with 1 tablespoon of rice vinegar and mix until evenly coated.

Step 4: In a separate pan, heat the oil. Add the red pepper flakes, garlic, ginger, and green onion and stir-fry for 30 seconds until fragrant.

Step 5: Stir in the honey, remaining salt, rice vinegar, and soy sauce, mixing until well combined.

Step 6: Pour the sauce over the lotus root salad, tossing to mix well.

Step 7: Garnish with extra chopped green onions or sesame seeds.

Caprese Salad

My husband has an infatuation with tomatoes. Ever since we started dating, he would pick up a basket of tomatoes at the market. When it comes to selecting the perfect tomato, he can be a bit obsessive. He knows that the best ones are grown in rich, loamy soil and ripened on the vine for maximum sweetness. He can tell at a glance whether a tomato is perfectly ripe or still needs a few days to reach its full potential.

That is why every time we make this salad, I see his eyes light up with excitement. Caprese salad is a beautiful and simple dish that can be prepared with ease. Crafting this classic favorite takes mere minutes, making it ideal for those short on time but still wanting the burst of flavor that a delicious salad can bring.

Ingredients:
This will make 2 portions.
2 medium-sized ripe tomatoes (about 400 g)
4 ounces of fresh mozzarella cheese (about 113 g)
8–10 large fresh basil leaves
1 tablespoon of high-quality extra-virgin olive oil (15 ml)
1 tablespoon of balsamic vinegar (15 ml)
salt and freshly ground black pepper to taste

Steps:

Step 1: Slice tomato into quarter-inch-thick rounds. Place the tomato slices on a serving plate.

Step 2: Slice the mozzarella cheese into quarter-inch-thick rounds and place them on top of the tomato slices. Alternate between the tomato and mozzarella.

Step 3: Chiffonade the basil leaves (cut them into long, thin strips, as if you were cutting ribbons) and sprinkle them over the mozzarella slices.

Step 4: Drizzle the extra-virgin olive oil and balsamic vinegar over the entire salad.

Step 5: Season with salt and freshly ground black pepper to taste.

Step 6: Serve immediately and enjoy!

Tips:

- If you don't have whole tomatoes, cherry tomatoes work great in caprese salad. They have a similar flavor and texture to regular tomatoes and are often sweeter.
- When selecting tomatoes for salad, look for ones that are firm and have a bright color. Avoid any that are mushy or have bruises or cracks.
- It's best not to refrigerate tomatoes, as it can cause them to lose their flavor and texture. Instead, store them at room temperature and use them within a few days.

Pesto Pasta Salad

Over time, pesto has become one of the most popular sauces in the world, enjoyed by both home cooks and professional chefs alike. Whether stirred into pasta or used as a spread for sandwiches, pesto adds a bright, flavorful twist to any dish. The delightful blend of pasta and luscious pesto sauce creates an enchanting blend of warm flavors; salty and rich with just the right amount of acidity. It can also be made ahead of time and stored. This pesto pasta salad is the perfect dish for a summer picnic.

Ingredients:
1 cup roasted cherry tomatoes (about 150 g)
½ cup cucumber (75 g)
½ red bell pepper (75 g)
2 tablespoons olive oil (30 ml)
½ cup sun-dried tomato (55 g)
8 ounces bowtie pasta (about 227 g)
salt
freshly ground black pepper
For the pesto sauce:
2 cups fresh basil leaves (about 45 g)
½ cup olive oil (a120 ml)
½ cup Parmesan cheese (55 g)
¼ cup pine nuts (40 g)
3 cloves garlic

Steps:

Step 1: Preheat your oven to 375°F (190°C).

Step 2: Cut the cherry tomatoes in half and place them on a baking sheet lined with parchment paper. Drizzle olive oil over the tomatoes and sprinkle with salt and pepper.

Step 3: Roast the cherry tomatoes in the preheated oven for 15 to 20 minutes or until they are slightly caramelized.

Step 4: Cut the cucumber and bell pepper into small bite-sized pieces and set aside.

Step 5: While the tomatoes are roasting, make the pesto. Add the basil leaves, olive oil, Parmesan cheese, pine nuts, garlic, salt, and pepper to a food processor or blender.

Step 6: Blend the ingredients until they are well combined and the sauce has reached your desired consistency. If the sauce is too thick, you can add additional olive oil until it reaches the desired consistency.

Step 7: Taste the sauce and adjust the seasoning as necessary. Add additional salt and pepper if needed.

Step 8: Cook the pasta in a large pot of boiling water according to the package directions.

Step 9: Once the pasta is cooked, drain it and rinse with cool water, then return it to the pot. Add the pesto sauce and stir until well combined. Toss roasted cherry tomatoes, sun-dried tomatoes, cucumber, and red bell pepper in.

Step 10: Serve the pasta with additional Parmesan cheese and black pepper, if desired.

Lemon Pasta Salad

The pasta salad is a classic picnic dish—and for good reason. It's easy to prepare, transport, and serve, and can be made ahead of time. This lemon pasta salad is a particular favorite, thanks to its zesty flavor and bright color. This dish combines the tangy taste of lemon with the freshness of crisp vegetables. When it comes to picnic fare, few dishes are as satisfying as a flavorful lemon pasta salad.

Ingredients:
This will make 4 servings as a side.
2 lemons, juiced (90–120 ml)
8 ounces of farfalle pasta (227 g)
½ cucumber, sliced
1 cup cherry tomatoes, halved (150 g)
¼ cup olives, sliced (30 g)
1 small shallot, finely chopped (20–30 g)
2-3 tablespoons olive oil (30—45 ml)
small handful of fresh basil, chopped
1 clove garlic, minced
1 teaspoon Dijon mustard (5 ml)
¼ cup freshly grated Parmesan cheese (about 30 g)
salt and pepper to taste

Steps:

Step 1: For the dressing: Mince garlic. Zest and squeeze lemons into a bowl with shallots, minced garlic, Dijon mustard, olive oil, salt, and pepper. Whisk until combined.

Step 2: Boil farfalle pasta until al dente. Rinse with cold water to stop cooking and drain.

Step 3: Cut the cherry tomatoes, cucumber, and basil.

Step 4: In a large mixing bowl, combine the dressing with pasta and cherry tomatoes, cucumber, olives, and basil. Mix and top with Parmesan. Season with salt and pepper.

Rice *and* Noodles

Kimbap

As I walked to the grove, I could not help but feel excitement at the thought of sharing my kimbap with my friends. We laughed with the gentle wind blowing against our faces, smiling at this little moment in time.

Kimbap is a delicious Korean dish that can be enjoyed at any time of day. They are an exceptionally popular picnic dish because they are easy to make and can be customized to suit any taste. The colors of the kimbap, from the bright yellow of the pickled radish to the green of the spinach, are a feast for the eyes.

Ingredients:
This will make 4-6 rolls of kimbap for 2-3 servings.
2 cups of rice (400 g of rice)
4 ounces of spinach (about 113 g)
1 medium-sized carrot, julienned (60 g to 100 g, depending on the size)
4-6 strips of danmuji or pickled yellow radish[1]
4-6 strips of marinated burdock root
1 tablespoon of sesame oil (15 ml)
4-6 sheets of seaweed
pinch of sugar and salt

Steps:

Step 1: Cook the short-grain rice. You can use a rice cooker or cook over a stove.

Step 2: Once the rice has been cooked, evenly season it with 2 tablespoons of sesame oil and 1 tablespoon of salt.

Step 3: Next, prepare your ingredients. For the carrots: peel and thinly slice. Heat a bit of oil in a pan and sauté carrots until softened.

Step 4: For the spinach: blanch the spinach in a pot. Remove and strain. Toss the spinach with a bit of sesame oil and salt.

Step 5: Whisk eggs with a pinch of sugar and salt. Grease a small pan with oil. On medium heat, pour the egg mixture in until a thin layer forms. Flip once the egg has evenly cooked. Remove from heat and let cool. Slice into thin strips.

---

[1] The danmuji and burdock root typically comes in a pack you can find in any Korean grocery store.

Step 6: Next, it's time to roll the kimbap. Take out a sheet of seaweed with the shiny side face down. Place a thin layer of rice on three-fourths of the seaweed evenly.

Step 7: Place a row of spinach, carrot, yellow radish, burdock root, and egg close to the top of the rice, leaving a small gap.

Step 8: Roll the kimbap tightly all the way through. You can use a bamboo sushi mat to help keep the kimbap even and tightly rolled. This tool can make a huge difference. If you do not have one, you can omit and roll as tightly as you can.

Step 9: Season with a layer of sesame oil. When you are ready to serve, slice the kimbap into even-sized pieces and pack.

Tip: It is important that you do not refrigerate the kimbap, as the rice will harden. You must make kimbap the same day or it will not have the same texture.

Soothing Mushroom Rice

Autumn had arrived, and with it came a feeling of warmth and comfort. The air was crisp, the leaves were turning shades of orange and red, and there was a certain sense of stillness that only the change of seasons could bring. I was in my kitchen preparing something special—mushroom rice. I'd been wanting to make this dish for some time now; its warm yellow color reminded me of the sunsets. It's a warm and comforting dish ideal for any season, but perfect for fall weather. I worked away, chopping the uneven mushrooms and carrots, combining them into the rice. The rice cooked slowly but I was in no rush. As I took my first bite, savory earthy tones permeated through every spoonful—reminding me once again why autumn is such an extraordinary season in its own unique way.

Picture yourself sitting down to a warm, comforting bowl of rice infused with the earthy, delicate flavors of mushrooms. This dish soothes the soul and warms the heart, providing a sense of comfort with every bite.

Ingredients:
This will make 2 portions as a main dish or 3–4 as a side dish.
1 cup short-grain rice (200 g)
1½ cups water (355 ml)
2 tablespoons soy sauce (30 ml)
1 tablespoon mirin (15 ml)
1 tablespoon dashi powder or chicken bouillon powder (around 12 g)
½ tablespoon sugar (about 7 g)
1 tablespoon oil (15 ml)
1 cup mushrooms, sliced (such as shiitake, enoki, and shimeji) (90 g)
1 cup diced carrot (130 g to 150 g)
1 tablespoon finely minced ginger (8 g)
1 teaspoon sesame oil (5 ml)
2 green onions, chopped (20 g)
pinch of salt

Steps:

Step 1: Rinse the rice thoroughly in cold water until the water runs clear. Drain well.

Step 2: In a small bowl, combine the water, soy sauce, mirin, sugar, oil, ginger, and dashi powder. If you do not have dashi powder, you can substitute an equal amount of chicken bouillon powder. Stir until dissolved.

Step 3: In your rice cooker, combine the rice and wet ingredient mixture. Layer the mushrooms and carrots on top. Do not mix the mushrooms and carrots into the rice, as they will naturally mix in during the cooking process. Turn the rice cooker on.

If you do not have a rice cooker, add the same ingredients to a nonstick pot. Bring the mixture to a boil over high heat, then reduce the heat to low and cover with a lid. Let reduce for 12 to 15 minutes or until the water is fully evaporated.

Step 4: When the rice is ready, remove it from the heat and fluff. Add in the green onions, a pinch of salt, and stir well. Top with roasted seaweed and a drizzle of sesame oil.

Onigiri

Onigiri is a popular Japanese dish that consists of rice balls filled with a variety of ingredients, such as salmon, tuna, or pickled vegetables. It is a convenient and tasty treat that is perfect for picnics due to its compact size and portability. One of the great things about onigiri is that it can be customized to fit your taste preferences. Whether you prefer a simple salted rice ball or one that is filled with flavorful ingredients, onigiri offers something for everyone. So next time you're planning a picnic, consider adding onigiri to your basket for a delicious and easy-to-eat option.

Spicy Tuna Onigiri

The sun was starting to set, painting the sky in a beautiful array of oranges and pinks. I had just finished my shift at work and decided to stop by the park on my way home. I sat down on a bench and pulled out my snack. Inside were two rice balls, neatly wrapped in seaweed. I unwrapped one of them and took a bite. I watched as the sun slowly dipped below the horizon. It was a perfect way to end my day.

Ingredients:
Makes 2-4 onigiris
1 can tuna (about 5 ounces or 142 g)
1 tablespoon sriracha sauce (15 ml)
2 tablespoons Japanese mayo (30 ml)
1 tablespoon soy sauce (15 ml)
1 tablespoon furikake (about 10 g) (a mix of dried fish, sesame seeds, and various seasonings)
2 nori seaweed sheets
1 cup uncooked Japanese short-grain rice (about 200 g)
1¼ cups water (about 295 ml)
salt to taste

Steps:

Step 1: Rinse the rice in cold water until the water runs clear and drain. Cook rice in a rice cooker or on the stovetop.

Step 2: To create the spicy tuna filling, add tuna to a small bowl with soy sauce, sriracha, and mayo.

Step 3: Press the onigiri. If you have an onigiri mold, you can press the rice in it. If you don't - wet your hands to avoid sticking. Take a small handful of rice and shape it into a ball. Add the filling in the center and add more rice on top, forming a triangle shaped ball. Press tightly.

Step 4: Wrap a small piece of seaweed around the onigiri. Top with furikake.

Salted Salmon Onigiri

If you're looking for a tasty and easy-to-prepare snack, salted salmon onigiri could be the perfect choice. This Japanese delicacy consists of a ball of sticky rice, often seasoned with furikake (see Spicy Tuna Onigiri recipe), wrapped around a savory filling of salted salmon. The result is a satisfying and flavorful treat that's perfect for an on-the-go snack or a light lunch. While it may seem intimidating to make your own onigiri at home, it's surprisingly easy and can be customized to your tastes.

Ingredients:
Makes 2–4 onigiris
1 salmon fillet (about 6 ounces or 170 g)
1 tablespoon salt (about 17 g)
1–2 tablespoons sake or similar cooking wine (15—30 ml)
2 nori seaweed sheets
1 cup uncooked Japanese short-grain rice (about 200 g)
1¼ cups water (about 295 ml)
furikake

Steps:

Step 1: Rinse the rice in cold water until the water runs clear and drain. Cook rice in a rice cooker or on the stovetop.

Step 2: Prepare the salmon. Pat salmon dry with a paper towel. Patting the salmon dry will help it absorb the marinade better. Add the sake and salt to the salmon. Let it marinade for 30 minutes. Preheat the oven to 400°F (205°C).

Step 3: Remove the salmon filet from the marinade. Pat dry salmon again. Place the salmon filet on a baking sheet lined with parchment paper and bake for 10 to 12 minutes, or until the salmon is cooked through and flakes easily with a fork.

Step 4: When the salmon is done cooking, Remove the salmon from the oven and let it cool for a few minutes. Shred the salmon with a fork into small pieces.

Step 5: Press the onigiri. If you have an onigiri mold, you can press the rice in it. If you don't - wet your hands to avoid sticking. Take a small handful of rice and shape it into a ball. Add the filling in the center and add more rice on top, forming a triangle shaped ball. Press tightly.

Ume Onigiri

Ume, also known as pickled plum, is a popular Japanese condiment. The plum is harvested in the summer months and then pickled in salt and vinegar. The result is a tangy and sweet flavor that is both refreshing and intense. Ume can be enjoyed on its own or used as a seasoning for a variety of dishes, ranging from rice and noodle dishes to salads and cocktails. Its unique flavor and versatile nature make Ume a favorite.

Please note this onigiri will be very tart to those unaccustomed to the taste. It is after all—pickled!

Ingredients:
Makes 2-4 onigiris
2-4 pieces umeboshi (pickled plum), depending on taste
2 nori seaweed sheets
1 cup uncooked Japanese short-grain rice (about 200 g)
1¼ cups water (about 295 ml)
salt to taste

Steps:

Step 1: Pit the umeboshi and chop into small pieces.

Step 2: Prepare the rice. Rinse the rice in cold water until the water runs clear and drain. Cook rice in a rice cooker or on the stovetop.

Step 3: Stir the umeboshi mixture into the rice until evenly coated. This will distribute the flavor evenly.

Step 4: Press the onigiri. If you have an onigiri mold, you can press the rice in it. If you don't - wet your hands to avoid sticking. Take a small handful of rice and shape it into a ball. Press tightly.

Step 5: Wrap a strip of seaweed around each onigiri. If you like, you can place a small piece of umeboshi on top for a decorative touch.

Inari Sushi

On days when I'm feeling a bit relaxed, I always think of inari. These deep-fried bean curds are a pantry staple as they're incredibly versatile.

Inari sushi is a popular Japanese dish made with rice and wrapped in a fried tofu pouch. Though it is often enjoyed as a quick snack, inari sushi is also a popular choice for bento boxes and special occasions. It's a beautiful delicacy that can be shared among family, friends and acquaintances. Because it comes in convenient rice parcels, it's also incredibly easy to eat. Inari sushi is effortless to pick up with chopsticks or hands making it appealing for any gathering.

Ingredients:
8 inari pockets (aburaage)
2 cups rice (400 g)
2¼ cups water (535 ml)
1 tablespoon sugar (15 g)
1 tablespoon mirin (15 ml)
1 tablespoon soy sauce (15 ml)
3 tablespoons rice vinegar (45 ml)
½ teaspoon salt (2.5 g)
For the toppings and sauce:
¼ cup green onion (25 g)
1 tablespoon soy sauce (15 ml)
1 tablespoon Japanese mayo (15 ml)
1 tablespoon sriracha (15 ml)

Steps:

Step 1: To make the sushi rice, rinse the rice in cold water and drain. Cook rice in a rice cooker.

Step 2: If you do not have a rice cooker, add the rice to a saucepan with equal parts water. Bring the mixture to a boil over medium heat. Reduce the heat to low and simmer until water is absorbed. Remove the pan from the heat and let it sit for 10 minutes. Once the rice is cooked, let it cool for a few minutes so that it is easier to handle and fluff.

Step 3: Add the rice vinegar, sugar, and salt to the rice. Mix well, making sure that the grain is evenly coated, and set aside.

Step 4: To make the dressing, combine the sriracha, mayo, and soy sauce.

Step 5: Chop the green onions well.

Step 6: Blot the pre-marinated inari pouches. You can also rinse them in water and blot for less marinade.

Step 7: To assemble the inari sushi, stuff each inari skin with the cooked sushi rice. Then, drizzle the spicy sriracha mixture on and top with green onion.

Easy Japchae

Japchae, a popular Korean dish, is a blend of various ingredients that contribute to its unique flavor and texture. The dish is traditionally served as a starter or side dish, and its popularity has made it a staple in Korean cuisine. Japchae is colorful and its varied ingredients are expertly combined to create a visually pretty dish. The dish is typically made using a combination of sweet potato starch noodles, various vegetables such as spinach, carrots, and mushrooms, and a range of proteins such as beef, pork, and shrimp. You can customize your japchae with your favorite ingredients.

Ingredients:
This will make 2-4 servings.
6 ounces sweet potato starch noodles (about 170 g)
4–5 shiitake mushrooms, sliced
½ small onion, sliced (70 g)
¼ red bell pepper, sliced thinly (45 g)
¼ yellow bell pepper, sliced thinly (45 g)
2 cups spinach (60 g)
½ carrot, julienned (65 g)
2 garlic cloves, minced (8 g)
2 tablespoons soy sauce (30 ml)
2 tablespoon sesame oil (30 ml)
1 tablespoon vegetable oil (15 ml)
1 tablespoon sugar (15 g)
salt
black pepper

Steps:

Step 1: Cook the sweet potato noodles according to the package instructions. Drain and rinse them in cold water. In a large bowl, toss with 1 tbsp of sesame oil so the noodles do not stick together, then set aside.

Step 2: In a large pan or wok over medium-high heat, sauté the mushrooms and onions with a tablespoon of vegetable oil until they are soft and slightly browned. Add to the bowl with noodles.

Step 3: Add the bell peppers, carrots, and garlic to the pan and stir-fry for another 2 to 3 minutes until the vegetables are tender. Add to the bowl.

Step 4: Blanch the spinach for 30 seconds, then squeeze the excess water out. Add to the bowl. Stir all the ingredients together to make sure it's evenly mixed.

Step 5: In a separate bowl, mix together the soy sauce, sesame oil, sugar, salt, and pepper. Once combined, pour the sauce over the vegetables and noodles and stir until everything is coated evenly.

Step 6: Garnish with chopped green onions and sesame seeds.

Sandwiches *and* Wraps

Smoked Salmon Bagel *with* Lox *and* Cream Cheese

A simple breakfast staple—lox and cream cheese atop the perfectly toasted bagel. Simple and easy to whip up in less than 10 minutes, this recipe is sure to get you out the door quickly.

Ingredients:
This will make 2 servings.
2 bagels
4–8 ounces smoked salmon (about 113 g to 227 g)
2 tablespoons capers (30 g)
2 ounces cream cheese (about 57 g)
1 small red onion (about 100 g)
fresh dill (optional)
salt and pepper to taste

Steps:

Step 1: Cut the bagels in half and toast them until golden brown.

Step 2: Spread a generous amount of cream cheese over the top half of each bagel.

Step 3: Arrange the smoked salmon and distribute it evenly over the bagel. Thinly slice the red onion and sprinkle it over the bagel.

Step 4: Sprinkle the capers on top. Season with salt and pepper to taste.

Step 5: If desired, garnish with fresh dill leaves.

Cucumber Tea Sandwich

I quietly sipped on my freshly steeped tea, hands warm against my cup, and I looked over at my friends. Our afternoon tea was an array of scrumptious delicacies, from sweet scones to savory cucumber sandwiches.

Delightfully fresh and tantalizingly crisp, cucumber sandwiches are an exquisite afternoon snack that can be enjoyed by everyone.

Ingredients:
This will make 2-3 servings.
½ medium cucumber
4–6 slices of white or whole wheat bread (depending on how many sandwiches you want to make)
butter (softened) for spreading to taste
Optional: cream cheese or herbed spread (if you prefer a creamier filling)

Steps:

Step 1: Start by thinly slicing a cucumber lengthwise using a mandolin or a sharp knife.

Step 2: Spread butter on one side of each slice of bread. Place the cucumber slices on top of the buttered bread, and then top with another slice of bread.

Step 3: Use a serrated knife to trim the crusts off of the sandwiches. For a more elegant presentation, cut each sandwich triangle in half diagonally.

Step 4: Serve with your favorite tea!

Katsu Sandwich

The katsu sandwich is a Japanese dish made with breaded and deep-fried pork, typically served with cabbage, pickles, and a sweet and tangy sauce. The dish has become increasingly popular in recent years.

To really make this recipe stand out, try to source Japanese Shokupan bread. It has a very soft and fluffy texture and a slightly sweet flavor, which comes from the addition of sugar or honey. This gives it a distinct taste that sets it apart. If you are unable to find this type of bread, you can also use any thick cut white bread.

Ingredients:
This will make 2 servings.
2 pork chops, boneless
1 cup of shredded cabbage (90 g)
1 cup of panko breadcrumbs (about 75 g)
½ cup of all-purpose flour (65 g)
2 large eggs, beaten
4 slices of shokupan bread or thick-cut white bread
frying oil (quantity will vary based on the size of your skillet)
1 tablespoon of Dijon mustard (15 g)
4 tablespoons of katsu sauce (65 g)
salt and pepper to taste

Steps:

Step 1: Wrap the pork in cling wrap and gently pound your pork chop with a meat mallet to tenderize. This will make the meat soft. Season both sides generously with salt and pepper.

Step 2: For the breading: place flour, eggs, and panko breadcrumbs into three separate dishes. Whisk the eggs with salt. Season the panko with salt and pepper.

Step 3: Coat the pork chop cutlets first in the flour, then egg, then the panko mixture.

Step 4: Fry the meat in oil until it is golden brown and cooked through. Alternatively, if you want to use the air fryer, set the temperature for 375°F and fry for 10 minutes, flipping once at the 5-minute mark.

Step 5: Set the pork chop aside to cool and crisp up.

Step 6: Thinly slice your cabbage.

Step 7: Assemble your sandwich. On one side of the bread, put Dijon mustard. Add the cabbage and pork chop to the sandwich. Drizzle with katsu sauce.

Step 8: Cut the edges from the sandwich and wrap in parchment paper.

Japanese Egg Sandwich

The bread was pillowy soft, with just the right amount of chewiness. The eggs were silky smooth, immaculately cooked to perfection. The spring breeze that gently caressed my face carried with it a hint of fresh blossom fragrance. I took a bite of my Japanese egg sandwich and felt a smile slowly form.

Ingredients:
This will make 2 servings.
4–5 large eggs
¼ cup Japanese mayonnaise (55 g)
2 tablespoons of cream (30 ml)
a pinch of salt and sugar
4 slices of soft white bread

Steps:

Step 1: Hard-boil the eggs, then peel and chop them.

Step 2: In a bowl, mix together the chopped eggs, mayonnaise, cream, sugar, salt, and pepper.

Step 3: Butter the bread, then spread the egg mixture on top.

Step 4: Cut the crust of the sandwich and cut diagonally. Wrap in parchment paper.

Ham and Cheese Croissant

There's nothing quite like a classic ham and cheese croissant. The perfect picnic food, it's simple yet flavorful and always satisfying. The key to a good croissant is that it should be freshly baked, soft and flakey, with a crisp, crusty exterior.

Ingredients:
This will make 2 servings.
4 ounces ham (113 g)
4 slices sharp cheddar
2 croissants
1 tablespoon Dijon mustard (15 g)
1 tablespoon mayonnaise (15 g)
2 cups arugula (about 50 g)
1 tablespoon olive oil (15 ml)
1 tablespoon lemon juice (15 ml)
salt and pepper to taste

Steps:

Step 1: In a bowl, toss the arugula in olive oil, lemon juice, salt, and pepper.

Step 2: Cut the croissant open. Spread each side with a thin layer of Dijon mustard and mayonnaise.

Step 3: Arrange the ham and sharp cheddar on the croissant. Layer the arugula on top.

Caprese Sandwich

If you have never had a caprese sandwich, you are truly missing out on something special. The caprese sandwich is a type of Italian sandwich, made with fresh mozzarella, tomatoes, and basil. It is usually made with a type of white bread, such as ciabatta or baguette, but can also be made with other types of bread, such as focaccia. The various flavors come together in perfect harmony, mixing for an unforgettable experience.

Ingredients:
This will make 2 servings.

4 slices of your favorite bread (sourdough and Italian work great!)
2 tablespoons olive oil (30 ml)
2 tablespoons balsamic vinegar (30 ml)
6 slices of tomato (about 120 g)
6 ounces fresh mozzarella cheese (about a half-inch thick, about 170 g)
fresh basil leaves
salt and pepper to taste

Steps:

Step 1:. Brush each side of bread with olive oil and toast until golden brown.

Step 2: Lay one slice of toasted bread on a flat surface and top with sliced tomato, mozzarella cheese, and basil leaves (if using).

Step 3: Sprinkle salt and pepper, to taste.

Step 4: Drizzle with balsamic vinegar.

Step 5: Top with the other piece of toast and press down lightly so that the two halves stick together firmly.

Step 6: Wrap in parchment paper. Cut in half and enjoy!

Prosciutto, Fig, and Brie Sandwich

There are very few sandwiches that are universally loved. And I found this particular one is a crowd favorite. Crafted with little effort, the prosciutto, fig, and Brie sandwich requires minimal skill to assemble. It's quick to make and delicious as well. Sweet and salty collide in this delightful sandwich, perfectly balancing the tartness of fig jam with the richness of prosciutto.

Ingredients:

4 slices bread (sourdough or French bread recommended)
4–6 slices prosciutto
4–6 fresh figs, sliced
4 ounces Brie cheese, sliced (113 g)
1 cup arugula (about 25 g)
1 tablespoon balsamic vinegar (15 ml)
2 tablespoons extra-virgin olive oil (30 ml)
2 tablespoons fig preserves or honey (40 ml)
salt and pepper to taste

Steps:

Step 1: First, toss arugula with a squeeze of olive oil, balsamic vinegar, salt, and pepper.

Step 2: Cut the French baguette in half. Spread fig preserves on both sides of the bread.

Step 3: Cut the Brie into even pieces. Cut figs in half. Assemble the Brie, prosciutto, sliced figs, and arugula onto the sandwich. Drizzle with balsamic vinegar.

Step 4: Add a pinch of salt and pepper.

Step 5: Wrap the sandwich in parchment paper and twine.

Strawberry Cream Sandwich

Vibrant colors and delightful smells, each more heavenly than the last, filled the tiny Japanese convenience store. I immediately made my way to the perfectly lined sandwich shelf. Before long, my gaze fell upon the fresh cream and strawberry sandwiches.

The delicate balance between soft, fluffy bread and sweet, flowery strawberries created a delicate flavor unlike anything I've had before.

Ingredients:
6–9 fresh strawberries
4 slices milk bread or any soft bread
1 cup heavy cream (240 ml)
3 tablespoons sugar (40 g)

Steps:

Step 1: Choose fresh, ripe strawberries. Cut off the stem and leaves.

Step 2: Make the whipped cream. Combine heavy cream and sugar. Whisk until stiff peaks form.

Step 3: Spread a layer of whipped cream on one slice of bread. Place the strawberries on top in a diagonal pattern across the sandwich.

Step 4: Add a second layer of whipped cream on top of the strawberries. The cream should cover the strawberries entirely.

Step 5: Place the other slice of bread on top of the sandwich. Wrap tightly with cling wrap and refrigerate for an hour until the cream hardens.

Step 6: Cut off the crusts and slice vertically, revealing the strawberry center. Serve immediately or refrigerate until ready to serve.

Mini Focaccia Pizzas

The kitchen was bustling with activity as I set out to make the perfect mini focaccia pizzas. I began by gathering all the necessary ingredients—olive oil, garlic, cherry tomatoes, colorful bell peppers, fresh basil, and of course, cheese.

I expertly stretched the dough out, ensuring that each mini focaccia was of uniform size and thickness. With a painter's precision, I brushed each little pizza with fruity olive oil, covering every inch of the bread with its golden sheen. Into the oven they went. As I watched each mini focaccia bubble and crisp up, the heady aroma of baked cheese and basil made my senses tingle with excitement. Nothing is more fun than decorating these mini focaccia pizzas.

Focaccia pizza is the perfect indulgence. This tasty treat combines the ease of a classic pizza dough with the delicious aromas and punchy flavors of artisan bread. Every bite is filled with herby charred vegetables combined with salty meats, drizzled with extra-virgin olive oil.

Ingredients:
This will make 1-2 medium pizzas for 2-3 servings.

½ package (about 1 teaspoon) active dry yeast (2.8 g)
½ cup warm water (120 ml)
1 tablespoon sugar (14 g)
1½ cups all-purpose flour (180 g)
½ teaspoon salt (3 g)
2 tablespoons olive oil (30 ml)

For the toppings:
½ cup pizza sauce (120 ml)
1 cup shredded mozzarella cheese (about 100 g)
½ red bell pepper, thinly sliced (70 g)
½ yellow bell pepper, thinly sliced (70 g)
½ small red onion, thinly sliced (50 g)
½ zucchini, thinly sliced (70 g)
1 small tomato, sliced (about 100 g)
a handful of spinach leaves (about 20 g)
¼ cup black olives, sliced (about 30 g)
fresh basil leaves for garnish

Steps:

Step 1: In a large bowl, combine the yeast, warm water, and sugar. Activate the yeast by letting it sit for about 5 minutes. It should be frothy.

Step 2: Add the flour and salt to the yeast mixture and mix. Add 1 tablespoon of the olive oil. Mix together to start forming a dough.

Step 3: Transfer the dough onto a floured surface and knead for about 5 to 7 minutes until it's smooth and elastic.

Step 4: Place the dough in a greased bowl, cover with a towel, and let it rise in a warm area for about an hour or until it doubles in size.

Step 5: Preheat your oven to 425°F (220°C).

Step 6: Punch down the dough to remove excess air and transfer to a greased baking sheet. Shape it into a rectangle, about a half-inch thick. Use your fingers to make dimples. Drizzle the remaining tablespoon of olive oil over the top.

Step 7: Spread the pizza sauce evenly over the dough, leaving a small border around the edges for the crust.

Sprinkle half of the mozzarella over the sauce. Then distribute the bell peppers, red onion, zucchini, tomato, spinach leaves, and olives over the cheese to form an attractive pattern. Sprinkle the rest of the mozzarella on top.

Step 8: Bake for about 15 to 20 minutes, or until the cheese is bubbly and golden, and the crust is lightly browned.

Step 9: Remove from the oven, let it cool slightly, then garnish with fresh basil leaves. Slice into squares or wedges, and enjoy your colorful and delicious focaccia pizza!

Mini Puff Pastry Bites

If a delicious yet effortless meal is what you seek for your outdoor gathering, look no further than these puff pastry bites! Puff pastry is an essential element in the baker's arsenal. Its golden, flaky layers add a lovely texture to a variety of sweet and savory dishes. This dish is extremely versatile—fillings can be adapted to suit any palate. Incorporating puff pastry into your baking repertoire is perfect for flavorful, yet effortless results.

Ingredients:
This will make 3-4 servings.
1 sheet frozen puff pastry, thawed
¼ cup grated Parmesan cheese (25 g)
½ cup cherry tomatoes (75—100 g)
1–2 shallots
a few sprigs of thyme
a few sprigs of basil
pesto
salt and pepper to taste

Steps:

Step 1: Preheat your oven to 400°F (205°C) and line your baking sheet with parchment paper.

Step 2: Roll out your thawed puff pastry into a thin layer. Cut the puff pastry into even squares.

Step 3: Drizzle olive oil onto the parchment paper. Layer shallots, cherry tomatoes, and Parmesan cheese on the sheet. Season with a few sprigs of thyme and a pinch of salt and pepper.

Step 4: Lay the puff pastry squares on top of the mixture. Crimp the edges with a fork so that it adheres. Brush a beaten egg on top if you want a more golden shell.

Step 5: Bake for 15 minutes or until all ingredients are cooked through.

Step 6: Plate and add additional basil on top. Optionally, add a dollop of pesto.

Desserts

Cherry Pie

There's nothing quite like a slice of cherry pie. The flaky crust, the tart filling, the juicy cherries. And when it's made with love, it's even more special. When you take a bite, you can just feel the summertime sunshine on your face. Whether you're picnicking in the park or in your own backyard, cherry pie is sure to make it feel like a perfect summer day.

Ingredients:
This will make 1 medium to large cherry pie with 8 servings.
For the pie crust:
2½ cups all-purpose flour (312 g)
1 teaspoon salt (5 g)
1 teaspoon sugar (5 g)
1 cup unsalted butter, cold and cut into small cubes (227 g)
¼ to ½ cup ice water (60–120 ml)
For the cherry filling:
4 cups fresh cherries, pitted (600 g)
½ to ¾ cup sugar (about 100–150 g; adjust based on the sweetness of the cherries and your preference)
1 tablespoon fresh lemon juice (15 ml)
2 tablespoons cornstarch (15 g)
¼ teaspoon vanilla extract (1 ml)
For the egg wash:
1 egg, beaten
1 tablespoon milk or cream (15 ml)
sugar for sprinkling (optional)

Steps:

Step 1: First, let's make the pie crust. In a large bowl, combine the flour, salt, and sugar. Add the cold unsalted butter and blend into the flour mixture until coarse.

Step 2: Gradually add ¼ to ½ cup of ice water, mixing in one tablespoon at a time, just until the dough comes together.

Step 3: Divide the dough in half, flatten each half into a disk, wrap in plastic wrap, and refrigerate for at least an hour.

Step 4: Preheat your oven to 375°F (190°C).

Step 5: On a floured surface, roll out one of the dough disks into a twelve-inch circle. Carefully transfer it into a nine-inch pie dish. Gently press the dough into the bottom and sides of the dish. Trim any overhang.

Step 6: To par-bake the crust, line your pie crust with parchment paper or aluminum foil. Fill the crust with pie weights, dried beans, or uncooked rice to keep it from puffing up or shrinking.

Step 7: Bake the pie crust in your preheated oven for about 15 to 20 minutes. Carefully remove the pie weights and the parchment paper or foil, then bake for an additional 5 minutes until the bottom of the crust is just beginning to brown. Allow it to cool while you prepare the filling.

Step 8: To make the cherry filling, combine the cherries, sugar, lemon juice, cornstarch, and vanilla extract. Let it sit for 10 to 15 minutes to allow the flavors to combine.

Step 9: Pour the cherry filling into the par-baked pie crust, distributing it evenly.

Step 10: Roll out the second disk of dough and cut into strips to create a lattice top for the pie. Trim and crimp the edges.

Step 11: Mix together the egg and milk to make the egg wash. Brush the egg wash onto the top and edges of the pie crust. Sprinkle it with sugar, if desired.

Step 12: Place the pie on a baking sheet to catch any drips and bake for about 30 to 35 minutes or until the crust is golden. If the edges of the pie start browning too quickly, cover them with foil.

Please note that the final baking time may vary. You may need to bake longer than 35 minutes, depending on your oven and the thickness of your pie crust. Always watch your pie carefully toward the end of baking to prevent it from over-browning.

How to Make a Lattice Pattern:

Step 1: Lay half of the strips over the pie, evenly spaced.

Step 2: Fold back every other strip to the center, then place another strip perpendicular.

Step 3: Unfold the folded strips back over the center strip.

Step 4: Repeat this process, alternating the strips you fold back, until the lattice is complete.

Fruit Tarts

The air was hot and muggy. One of the hottest days of the year. I waited by the window in anticipation. Today was the day we would make fruit tarts.

This fruit tart is something special. A buttery and flaky crust is filled with a creamy custard filling, and then topped with an array of fresh fruits. The result is a tart that is both rich and refreshing, with a hint of sweetness from the fruit. This tart is best enjoyed on a warm day, with a cup of tea or coffee. It's the perfect way to enjoy the season's bounty.

These decadent fruit tarts are single-serving. There's something so satisfying about having your own personal fruit tart. Not to mention, single-serving fruit tarts are way easier to eat on the go. No forks or plates required.

Ingrediants:
Makes 4 small fruit tarts.

Crust:
1 stick butter (113 g)
¼ cup brown sugar (55 g)
1 cup flour (125 g)
¼ teaspoon salt (1.5 g)
¼ teaspoon baking powder (1.2 g)
½ teaspoon cinnamon (2 g)
1 egg

Custard:
4 tablespoons sugar (50 g)
2 cups whole milk (480 ml)
4 egg yolks
3 tablespoons cornstarch (25 g)
½ tablespoon vanilla extract (7.5 ml)

Fruit glaze:
½ cup apricot jam (about 160 g)
1 tablespoon water (15 ml)

Fruit to top:
½ cup fresh berries (about 70 g)
mint

Steps:

Make the tart crust:

Step 1: Preheat the oven to 375°F (190°C). Grease four small tart pans.

Step 2: Cream the butter and sugar. Add both to a large bowl or stand mixer and beat until fluffy.

Step 3: In another bowl, sift flour with salt, cinnamon, and baking soda.

Step 4: Combine the flour, egg, and butter mixture together slowly until dough forms.

Step 5: Chill the dough for 30 minutes to one hour.

Step 6: When the dough is ready, separate it into four small portions. Roll the dough out and press it into the tart mold. To get a nice edge, start by rolling a long piece. Press this piece along the side of the tart pan. Then roll a thin disk for the bottom. Use a small measuring cup dusted with flour to flatten the bottom, pressing along the sides to get that sharp edge.

Step 7: Prick pastry several times with a fork. To prevent the tart crust from rising, line the top with parchment paper and pie weights. Bake for 20 minutes until the tart crust turns golden brown. Allow to cool completely.

Make the custard:

Step 1: Pour milk, half the sugar, and vanilla extract into a saucepan. Cook over medium heat until it just starts to steam. Do not overcook.

Step 2: Whisk the egg yolks in a bowl with the cornstarch and half the sugar until smooth. Slowly pour the warm milk into the egg yolk mixture while whisking. Be careful to add it in slowly so it does not cook.

Step 3: Transfer the mixture back to the saucepan over medium heat. Bring it to a slow boil while whisking continuously.

Step 4: The custard should be thick at this point. Transfer to a bowl and store in the fridge until chilled.

Make the glaze:

Step 1: In a saucepan, combine the jam and water. Heat on medium heat.

Step 2: Reduce until thickened.

Assembling the tart:

Step 1: Move the tart shells to a serving plate or container for transport.

Step 2: Layer in the custard cream.

Step 3: Arrange the fruit in an attractive manner on top of the custard. I recommend alternating berries to make a circle pattern.

Step 4: Brush the glaze on top for a shiny finish and garnish with sprigs of mint.

Croffles *with* Whipped Cream Cheese *and* Strawberries

The smell of freshly brewed coffee and baked goods filled the air of the tiny coffee shop. It was a cozy place, with warm golden lights and comfy armchairs tucked away in hidden nooks. I had heard about their newest treat, a croffle—a hybrid between a croissant and waffle—and I had yet to try one myself.

Taking my first bite, I felt like I was transported to another world: it was delightfully flaky and slightly crisp. As I savored every bit of that deliciousness, warmth spread through my body and made me feel right at home. Except I wanted more! I wanted to learn how to make this delicious concoction.

This twist on traditional French pastry requires only a waffle iron and a few simple ingredients. Croffles are also endlessly customizable, allowing you to experiment with sweet toppings.

Ingredients:
This will make about 4 servings.
½ package frozen croissant dough
cooking spray, for the waffle iron
½ cup whipped cream cheese (115 g)
2 tablespoons honey or powdered sugar (30 ml, adjust to taste)
½ cup mixed fresh berries (about 75 g, strawberries, blueberries, and raspberries)

Steps:

Step 1:   Preheat your waffle maker according to its instructions.

Step 2:   While your waffle maker is preheating, lightly flatten your croissants. You don't want them to be too thin, just enough to fit in your waffle maker.

Step 3:   Once the waffle maker is ready, lightly coat it with cooking spray or butter.

Step 4:   Place a croissant on the waffle iron and close. Cook the croissant until it's golden brown and crispy. This should take about 3 to 4 minutes, but times may vary depending on your waffle maker.

Step 5:   While the croissants are cooking, whip together the cream cheese and honey (or powdered sugar) until it's light and fluffy. Put the cream cheese mixture in a piping bag.

Step 6:   Once the croffles are done, carefully remove them from the waffle maker and let them cool slightly on a wire rack. Once cooled, pipe the cream cheese mixture on top.

Step 7:   Top your croffles with the mixed fresh berries.

Chocolate Strawberries

Chocolate-dipped strawberries are the perfect indulgence for any occasion. First, the rich flavor of chocolate enhances the sweetness of the berries, creating a heavenly combination. The contrast in textures is also delightful, with the smooth chocolate coating giving way to the juicy flesh of the fruit. And finally, they are simply beautiful to look at, with the bright red berries peeking out from a pool of dark chocolate.

Ingredients:
This will make 8–10 chocolate strawberries.
4 ounces chocolate chips of your choice (113 g)
8–10 fresh strawberries

Steps:

Step 1: Wash the strawberries and dry completely. Any moisture will prevent the chocolate from adhering and hardening correctly.

Step 2: Heat the chocolate in a double boiler: place one bowl of hot water and another bowl with the chocolate directly above it. The steam from the water should melt the chocolate. Don't get any water in the chocolate or it won't harden correctly.

Step 3: Peel the leaves of the strawberries back. You can also use a skewer for easier dipping if needed. Dip the strawberries into the chocolate. Let each sit separately on parchment paper to harden.

Step 4: Optional: drizzle with white chocolate or sprinkles.

Lemon Tart

With every breath, sweet lemony notes wafted around, enveloping all who stepped inside with cozy calmness.

The taste of a lemon tart is simply divine. Sweet, zingy and light, the vibrant citrus flavor transports a lucky few to a bright and sunny paradise. There's no denying that this dessert is an excellent option for every gathering—its tangy sweetness satisfies even the most selective palates. This lemon tart recipe is perfect for novice bakers as it requires little prep work. It's light, refreshing, and looks like a piece of art with beautiful toppings.

Ingredients:
This will make 1 lemon tart with 6–8 servings.

For the crust:
1½ cups graham cracker crumbs (170 g)
6 tablespoons of unsalted butter, melted (85 g)
¼ cup of sugar (50 g)
zest of 1 lemon

For the filling:
1 cup of heavy cream (240 ml)
8 ounces of cream cheese, softened (227 g)
½ cup of powdered sugar (65 g)
¼ cup of fresh lemon juice (60 ml)
1 teaspoon of vanilla extract (5 ml)

For the toppings:
fresh mint leaves
fresh blueberries
lemon slices

Steps:

Step 1:. Preheat the oven to 350°F (175°C) and begin by making the crust. In a mixing bowl, combine the graham cracker crumbs, melted butter, sugar, and lemon zest. Mix until everything is well combined.

Step 2: Lightly grease the tart pan. Press the crumb mixture evenly into the bottom and sides of a tart pan. Make sure to press the crust firmly and evenly to avoid any cracks or uneven surfaces. You can use the bottom of a measuring cup or glass to press the crust into the pan.

Step 3: Bake the crust for 10 minutes or until golden brown. Remove the tart crust from the oven and wait for it to cool completely. Put it in the refrigerator to quicken the process.

Step 4: Next, whip the heavy cream in a separate mixing bowl until stiff peaks form. Set aside.

Step 5: In a different bowl, beat the softened cream cheese and powdered sugar until smooth and creamy. Add the lemon juice and vanilla extract and mix well.

Step 6: Gently fold the whipped cream into the cream cheese mixture until everything is well combined.

Step 7: Remove the tart crust from the refrigerator and pour the lemon filling into the crust. Use a spatula to smooth out the top, creating an even surface.

Step 8: Now, it's time to decorate the tart. Arrange the mint leaves, blueberries, and lemon slices.

Step 9: Chill the tart for at least 2 to 3 hours, or until set. Once ready, remove it from the tart pan, slice it, and serve.

Strawberry Waffles

I knew that soon enough, the sweet aroma of freshly baked waffles would permeate the air. Finally, the moment arrived. I took a deep breath, opened the waffle iron, and there they were. Golden brown waffles, perfectly crisp on the outside and fluffy on the inside, just waiting to be devoured.

These miniature waffles have a crispy exterior and a fluffy interior. The individual portion size is perfect for breakfast or sharing with friends on a picnic.

Ingredients:

This will make 4–5 standard size waffles or 8 mini waffles for 2–3 servings.

1 cup all-purpose flour (120 g)
1 tablespoon sugar (15 g)
2 teaspoons baking powder (10 g)
¼ teaspoon salt (1.5 g)
1 egg
1 cup whole milk (240 ml)
2 tablespoons melted butter (30 g)

Steps:

Step 1: Preheat your waffle maker to medium-high heat.

Step 2: In a large mixing bowl, whisk together the flour, sugar, baking powder, and salt.

Step 3: In a separate bowl, beat the egg and stir in the milk and melted butter.

Step 4: Add the wet ingredients to the dry mixture and mix until smooth. The mixture should be slightly runny.

Step 5: Use a bit of butter to grease your waffle maker. Pour a generous scoop (about ¼ cup) of the batter onto each waffle mold.

Step 6: Cook for about 4 to 5 minutes or until the waffles are golden brown. If you are using an automatic waffle machine, the machine will shut off when each waffle is done cooking.

Step 7. Use a fork to gently remove the mini waffles. Wait until the waffles are completely cool before packing. You can let them cool on a rack so they stay crisp before packing. Serve with fresh strawberries and whipped cream.

Be sure to pack the strawberries and whipped cream separately to keep the waffles from getting soggy during transportation.

Zesty Lemon Pound Cake

There are few desserts more tantalizing than a perfectly executed lemon cake. The fragrant zest of juicy lemons, combined with the rich sweetness of icing, creates a delightful treat that is hard to resist. The bright flavor of the citrus is a perfect balance to the richness of the cake, making it a mouthwatering dessert. Whether you enjoy it for afternoon tea or as a special treat, lemon cake is sure to please.

Ingredients:
This will make a four-inch small cake for 2–3 servings.

1 cup all-purpose flour (125 g)
½ teaspoon baking powder (2.5 g)
¼ teaspoon salt (1.5 g)
½ cup unsalted butter, at room temperature (113 g)
¾ cup granulated sugar (150 g)
2 large eggs
2 tablespoons fresh lemon juice (30 ml)
1 tablespoon lemon zest (5 g)
edible flowers for garnish

For the icing:
1 cup powdered sugar (120 g)
1–2 tablespoons fresh lemon juice (15–30 ml)

Steps:

Step 1: Preheat your oven to 350°F (175°C). Grease your four-inch cake mold with butter.

Step 2: In a medium bowl, sift the flour, baking powder, and salt together. Set aside.

Step 3: In a larger bowl, beat the butter and sugar until light and fluffy. Add in the eggs, one at a time, beating to make sure each egg is well incorporated. Then slowly mix in the lemon juice and zest.

Step 4: Gradually add the dry ingredients to the butter mixture. Stir until everything is mixed in.

Step 5: Pour the batter into the prepared cake mold, smoothing the top with a spatula.

Step 6: Bake for 40 to 50 minutes, or until a toothpick inserted into the center comes out clean.

Step 7: Let the cake cool for about 10 minutes, then remove from the mold and let it cool completely on a wire rack.

Step 8: While the cake is cooling, prepare the icing. In a small bowl, whisk together the powdered sugar and 1 tablespoon of the lemon juice. If the icing is too thick, add more lemon juice, a teaspoon at a time, until you achieve a pourable consistency.

Step 9: Once the cake is completely cool, pour the icing over the top, letting it drip down the sides. It should harden.

Step 10: Decorate the top of the cake with edible flowers. Enjoy this beautiful and delicious lemon pound cake at your next picnic!

Note: Adjust baking times if necessary. Baking times can vary based on the specific size and material of your cake mold. If you notice the cake is browning too quickly, you can lightly cover it with foil.

Mini Strawberry Cakes

A strawberry cake is a truly indulgent dessert. The soft, luxurious texture of the spongy layers of cake mixed with the tart, juicy burst of sweet strawberries is an unforgettable combination. The delicate flavor of sweet strawberries merges with a light, fluffy sponge to create a sensation like floating on clouds. Imagine a soft sea of cream, blanketed in an effortless spiral of lush berries. Every bite reveals layers of moist cake and velvety creamy textures that are simply bursting with flavor.

Ingredients:
Makes 1 small four-inch cake.

For the cake:
- 1/3 cup cake flour (40 g)
- ¼ teaspoon baking powder (1.25 g)
- pinch of salt
- 3 tablespoons unsalted butter (42 g)
- 3 tablespoons whole milk (45 ml)
- 2 large eggs
- ½ cup granulated sugar (100 g)

For the filling:
- ¼ cup sugar syrup (¼ cup water + ¼ cup granulated sugar, boiled until sugar dissolves and the mixture thickens, about 60 ml after boiling)
- ½ cup sliced strawberries (75 g)
- ½ cup homemade whipped cream (120 g)
- additional strawberries for garnish

Steps:

Step 1: Make sure that the strawberries are thoroughly dried when making this cake. It is advised that the cake is made and eaten the same day, as it is delicate.

Step 2: Preheat your oven to 350°F (180°C). Grease one small four-inch cake pan well to avoid sticking.

Step 3: In a medium bowl, whisk together the dry ingredients.

Step 4: Separate your egg whites and yolks. Beat the egg yolks with sugar and milk until a ribbon forms when dropped from whisk. Whisk the egg whites to firm peaks. Slowly add the white to the yolk mixture, creating a meringue.

Step 5: Gradually sift the cake flour into the egg mixture while gently folding.

Step 6: Pour the batter into your greased cake pans.

Step 7: Bake the cake for 20 to 30 minutes, or until a toothpick inserted into the center comes out clean. If the cake is browning too quickly on top and not cooking in the middle, you can lightly cover with aluminum foil to prevent browning while the cake continues to bake.

Step 8: Let the cake cool for a few minutes. Slice the cake in half horizontally.

Step 9: Brush the sugar syrup on each cake layer. To assemble the cake, place one cake layer on a plate or cake stand. Spread a layer of whipped cream, then strawberries, then more whipped cream. Repeat with each layer.

Step 10: To finish, frost the sides and top of the cake with whipped cream and add strawberries to the top.

Strawberry Tanghulu

I could hardly contain my enthusiasm. Today was market day. Once a week my mother and I would stroll the street markets. Vendors would tout their goods in the open bazaar. Hundreds of stalls lined the street, selling everything from fresh produce to handmade goods.

As we walked through the bustling market, one stall caught my eye. I couldn't help but notice all of the colorful fruit. And then I saw it: strawberries crystallized on a beautiful skewer shimmering in the sunlight. As we walked home, I nibbled on the tanghulu. It was hard, crispy, and sweet all in one. And it was even better than I had imagined.

Whenever I make this treat, it always brings back memories of that special day with my mother.

Tanghulu, also known as candied fruit or sugar-coated hawthorn, is a popular Chinese street food made of fresh fruits skewered on bamboo sticks and dipped in hot syrup. The resulting treat is a crunchy, chewy, sweet-and-sour delight that is hard to resist.

While the traditional hawthorn fruit is still used in many cases, modern versions often feature a variety of different fruits, from strawberries and grapes to kiwis and bananas. In this recipe, we will be making tanghulu with strawberries, as they're more widely available.

Ingredients:
This will make 6–8 skewers.
2 cups sugar (400 g)
1 cup water (about 200 ml)
(the ratio is 2:1, so you can use any measurement you want!)
8–10 large strawberries
bamboo skewers
candy thermometer

Steps:

Step 1: Make sure that the fruit is washed and dried completely.

Step 2: Skewer the strawberries. I recommend three pieces per skewer to make sure that the berries are properly coated.

Step 3: In a pot over medium heat, combine the sugar and water.

Step 4: Use the candy thermometer to check the temperature. When the mixture reaches 300°F (150°C), coat the skewered strawberries in the mixture. Twirl to make sure all sides of the fruit are coated.

Step 5: The candy coating should harden instantly. If it feels soft or sticky, the mixture might not have been hot enough to harden.

Step 6: Let it harden on parchment paper, then store the tanghulu fruit side up. Best enjoyed the same day or immediately.

Tip:

- The sugar mixture is extremely hot, so please take care when handling. It's advisable to use a long-handled spoon or spatula and wear protective mitts during this process.
- Using a candy thermometer is crucial for ensuring the sugar solution reaches the hard-crack stage (300°F or 150°C).

Dango

These little spheres of goodness are a Japanese treat that have been around for centuries. Dango are made from mochiko or rice flour and are sometimes sweetened with honey or brown sugar. They are cooked on a skewer, three to four together. As they cook, bouncy, chewy texture forms. Sometimes dango are served plain, but often they are topped with green tea powder or sweet bean paste. No matter how they are enjoyed, dango is a delicious treat.

Hanami dango is said to represent the transient nature of the cherry blossoms, as they are only meant to be enjoyed for a short time. In Japan, hanami dango is often eaten while viewing the cherry blossoms, making it the perfect treat to enjoy during spring as the seasons change.

Ingredients:
This will make approximately 4–6 dango sticks with 3 balls each.
½ cup rice flour (80 g)
½ cup glutinous rice flour (80 g)
¼ teaspoon matcha powder or mugwort powder (1 g)
¼ teaspoon pink food coloring (1 g)
¼ cup sugar (50 g)
¼ cup of water (60 ml)

Steps:

Step 1: Mix rice flour, water, and sugar together in a bowl until it forms a dough.

Step 2: Separate the dough into three equal portions.

Step 3: Add matcha powder or mugwort powder to make the green dango. To make the pink dango, add a few drops of pink food coloring. Leave the third ball white.

Step 4: Then, take small pieces of the dough and roll them into balls, separating by color.

Step 5: In a pot, boil water. Cook the dango in order from lightest to deepest: white, then pink, then green.

Step 6: Once the balls start floating, remove and submerge in a cold ice bath. This will stop the cooking.

Step 7: Skewer the balls with your bamboo skewers.

Floral Sugar Cookies

As I opened up the kitchen windows, the warm rays of the sun enveloped my skin, and a gentle breeze danced through the air, carrying the sweet scent of blooming flowers and freshly cut grass. It was the perfect day for baking, and I couldn't wait to whip up some delicious sugar cookies.

Notes: By adding the flowers midway through baking, you can ensure that they keep more of their vibrancy. If you add the flowers in the beginning, they will fade a bit in color.

Ingredients:
This recipe makes two dozen sugar cookies.
½ cup unsalted butter, at room temperature (113 g)
½ cup granulated sugar (100 g)
1 large egg
1 teaspoon vanilla extract (5 ml)
1½ cups all-purpose flour (200 g)
¼ teaspoon baking powder (1 g)
a pinch of salt
fresh wild edible flowers for decoration

Steps:

Step 1: Preheat the oven to 375°F (190°C).

Step 2: In a large bowl, cream together the butter and sugar until light and fluffy. Beat in the eggs, one at a time, then stir in the vanilla extract. Sift together the flour, baking powder, and salt; gradually add to the creamed mixture until just blended.

Step 3: Refrigerate dough for at least 1 hour. Roll the dough out until an eighth-inch thick. Put dough on your baking sheet.

Step 4: Cut the cookies into desired shape with cookie cutter and remove excess.

Step 5: Bake for 8 minutes in the preheated oven, or until golden brown. Midway through baking, pull the cookies out and press the edible flowers into them. Return to the oven to complete baking. Cool on wire racks.

Step 6: Store in an airtight container.

Beverages

Sparkling Green Grape Ade

As I took my first sip, I was immediately taken aback by the unique flavor. There was a tart sweetness of the green grapes, balanced perfectly by the fizzy bubbles. I found myself lost in thought, enjoying the simplicity and charm of the moment. Here, in this little coffee shop, I found peace in the calming atmosphere and a new favorite drink to enjoy.

Ingredients:
This will make 2 servings.
2 cups green grapes (300 g)
¼ cup sugar (50 g)
½ cup water (120 ml)
1 tablespoon lemon juice (15 ml)
½ cup club soda (120 ml)
dehydrated lime slice

Steps:

Step 1: Begin by removing the stems from the green grapes. Add them to a blender and pulse until they are smooth.

Step 2: Strain the grape puree through a fine-mesh sieve into a mixing bowl, using a spoon to press the puree through the sieve.

Step 3: In a small saucepan, combine the water and sugar and heat over medium heat, stirring constantly until the sugar is dissolved. Remove from heat and allow to cool. You can store this mixture in the fridge and assemble the drink when you get to your location if necessary.

Step 4: Divide the grape mixture into two glasses filled with ice. Add sparkling water and lemon juice. Gently stir.

Step 5: Garnish the glasses with sliced green grapes and a slice of dehydrated lime.

Spiced Cider

As the crisp autumn air fills the air, many begin to crave the warm comfort of spiced cider. This delicious drink is made by simmering apples and spices in water, often with a bit of sugar or honey added to taste. The result is a fragrant, flavorful beverage that is perfect for chilly days.

Ingredients:
This will make 4 servings of spiced cider or 2 large servings.
4 cups apple cider (960 ml)
1 orange, sliced
1 lemon, sliced
1 cinnamon stick
2 teaspoons whole cloves (6 g)
2 teaspoons allspice berries (10 g)
1 teaspoon nutmeg (3 g)
½ cup brown sugar or ¼ cup honey (110 g)

Steps:

Step 1: In a large pot, combine the apple cider, orange slices, lemon slices, cinnamon stick, cloves, allspice berries, and nutmeg.

Step 2: Bring the mixture to a simmer over medium heat and then add the brown sugar or honey.

Step 3: Continue to simmer the cider until it is hot and the flavors have melded together, about 30 minutes.

Step 4: Serve the cider hot in mugs or cups and enjoy!

Strawberry Mint Spritz

The strawberry mint spritz is a refreshing and tantalizing drink that is perfect for any occasion. This drink combines the sweetness of strawberries with the cooling flavor of mint, all topped off with a sparkling bubbly finish. The beautiful pink hue of the drink is eye-catching and the bubbly feeling of the carbonation adds an extra touch of fun. Perfect for a summer picnic.

Ingredients:
This will make 2 servings.
4 large strawberries (72 g)
1 tablespoon sugar (15 g)
2 sprigs mint
16 ounces sparkling water (473 ml)

Steps:

Step 1: Cut and de-stem the strawberries. Place into a mortar with sugar and mint.

Step 2: Muddle the strawberry, sugar, and mint into a paste. Save until ready to consume.

Step 3: If desired, strain the mixture through a fine sieve to remove pulp and mint leaves.

Step 4: When ready to serve, divide the strawberry mixture between two glasses and top each with sparkling water.

Step 5: Garnish with a few slices of fresh berries and extra mint.

For a boozy twist, you can always add 1 to 2 ounces of your favorite alcohol.

Peach Bellini

The perfect picnic requires the perfect drink, and there is no more refreshing summer beverage than a peach Bellini. The delicate flavor of the peach is offset by the sweetness of the prosecco, and the subtle acidity of the wine helps to bring out the fruit's natural sweetness.

The color is a beautiful blush, similar to the skin of a ripe peach. When served chilled, the Bellini is refreshing and light, making it the perfect accompaniment to a summer meal. To make the most of this delicious drink, be sure to use ripe peaches and good-quality prosecco.

Ingredients:
This will make 3–6 servings.
1 bottle prosecco or 2 cans sparkling seltzer (750 ml)
2 white peaches
1 tablespoon sugar (15 g)
splash of lemon juice
mint or rosemary for garnish

Steps:

Step 1: To make the puree, start by peeling and chopping 2 ripe peaches. Reserve a few slices of peach for garnish.

Step 2: Add the peaches with sugar to a blender or food processor and blend until smooth. You should end up with about 1 cup of puree.

Step 3: When it is time to serve, fill each glass with the peach mixture, then top with prosecco. For a nonalcoholic option, top with sparkling seltzer.

Step 4: Garnish with a slice of fresh peach and enjoy!

Sparkling Lemonade

It was a beautiful day, the sort that begs you to spend it outdoors. And so my friend and I found ourselves enjoying sparkling lemonade on a patio, basking in the sunshine and relishing the peace of being surrounded by greenery. We laughed and chatted, taking occasional sips of our drinks and letting the sweetness wash over us.

Ingredients:
This will make 2–3 servings of lemonade.
½ cup lemon juice (120 ml)
½ cup sugar (about 100 g)
½ cup water (120 ml)
20 ounces sparkling water (about 590 ml)
ice
lemon slices and fresh mint for garnish

Steps:

Step 1: Create the simple syrup. In a small saucepan, heat the sugar and water over medium heat, stirring frequently, until the sugar has dissolved.

Step 2: Remove the pan from the heat and let the syrup cool completely.

Step 3: In a large pitcher, combine the syrup, freshly squeezed lemon juice, and sparkling water.

Step 4: Stir well and taste for sweetness. Add more syrup if desired.

Step 5: Fill glasses with ice and pour the lemonade. Garnish each glass with a slice of lemon and a sprig of fresh mint.

You can also add other fresh herbs or fruit slices before serving. Some good options include thyme, basil, and strawberries.

Strawberry Matcha Latte

The rich, earthy smell of matcha hits me. The matcha is a perfect shade of green, and the foam is thick and creamy. I take a sip, and the flavor is exactly what I hoped for—nutty and slightly sweet, with a hint of bitterness. It's the perfect pick-me-up, and I can't help but feel a sense of satisfaction.

Ingredients:
This will make 2-3 servings.
2 teaspoons matcha powder (10 g)
16 ounces milk of choice (475 ml)
2 teaspoons hot water (10 ml)
2 teaspoons sugar (8 g)
4 ounces of strawberry puree (about 115 g or 1 cup of fresh strawberries)
ice

For the strawberry puree:
1 cup fresh strawberries, hulled and quartered (about 150 g)
1–2 tablespoons sugar (15–30 g)

Steps:

For the strawberry puree:

Step 1: Place strawberries and sugar in a blender or food processor.

Step 2: Blend until smooth. Adjust sweetness if needed. Set aside.

For the matcha:

Step 1: In a small bowl, combine matcha powder and hot water. Whisk until the powder is fully dissolved and the mixture is frothy. Stir in sugar if desired.

Step 2: Pour equal amounts of strawberry puree into each glass.

Step 3: Add ice. Layer the matcha mixture over the strawberry puree.

Step 4: Pour the milk in, creating a beautiful, layered effect.

Rosemary Grapefruit Sparkler

The hazy sun was just beginning to set as we spread out the blanket on the soft, green grass. We slowly unpacked the wicker basket. The sweet-tart aroma of the grapefruit filled the air. Clinking our cups together, we settled back to enjoy the view. Sunlight danced through the leaves of the trees, casting a warm glow over everything.

Ingredients:
This will make 2 servings.
2 large grapefruits, peeled and segmented
¼ cup granulated sugar (50 g)
1 sprig fresh rosemary
8–10 ounces of sparkling water (about 240–295 ml)
ice

Steps:

Step 1: First, create the grapefruit puree jam. Begin by peeling and segmenting one large grapefruit. Save a few thin wedges for garnish. Place the grapefruit in a blender along with ¼ cup of sugar, ½ cup of water, and a pinch of salt. Blend until smooth and pour it into a small saucepan.

Step 2: Place the saucepan over medium-high heat and cook the grapefruit puree jam until it begins to thicken and reduces by half, approximately 10 to 15 minutes. Be sure to stir the jam often to prevent it from burning or sticking to the bottom of the pan.

Step 3: Once the grapefruit puree jam has finished cooking, let it cool to room temperature. Then, divide the jam evenly into two glasses. Top off with additional sparkling water.

Step 4: Garnish with fresh rosemary or your favorite garnish of choice and a slice of grapefruit.

Strawberry Milk

For someone looking to add a bit of sweetness and joy to their life, homemade strawberry milk is the perfect choice. It's a delicate and pretty drink that marries fragrant strawberries with creamy milk. For those who are dairy sensitive, you can substitute with any milk alternative.

Ingredients:
This will make 2 servings.
2 cups milk of choice (about 475 ml)
1 cup strawberries (150 g)
¼ cup sugar (50 g)

Steps:

Step 1: Cut the strawberries into small pieces. Discard stems.

Step 2: In a small pot, combine strawberries and sugar. Heat on low until syrup forms—about 10 to 15 minutes.

Step 3: Use a strainer or cheesecloth to strain the syrup.

Step 4: Add mixture to milk to create strawberry milk.

Ginger Peach Tea

Ginger peach tea is truly an elixir of delightful flavors. With its fragrant aroma, the sweet and spicy blend of ginger and peaches make each sip a sweet experience. It warms up the body like a hug from a loved one, filling you with comfort and happiness. Enjoyed either hot or cold, it's a delicious drink to soothe the soul. The fragrances expand in your tongue like a bouquet of flowers, the sweetness of the peach tea lightly accenting the earthy ginger taste.

Ingredients:
This will make 2 servings.
4–6 thin slices fresh ginger or one small knob
3 ripe peaches, peeled and sliced
4–6 tablespoons honey (or to taste, about 60–90 ml)
16 ounces water (475 ml)
fresh mint for garnish
1 tablespoon loose black tea or 2 teabags (about 15 g)
fresh mint for garnish

Steps:

Step 1: Prepare the tea and ginger. Peel and slice the ginger into thin pieces and add to the teapot. Place the loose black tea or tea bags in and add boiling water. Allow the tea to steep for 3 to 5 minutes. For a more intense ginger flavor, simmer for longer or add more.

Step 2: Once the tea has finished steeping, it is time to strain. To do this, simply place a strainer over a heat proof pitcher and pour the tea. This will remove any pieces of ginger or tea leaves. Set aside.

Step 3: Cut the peaches into small cubes and add to a saucepan with honey. Stir until the honey has dissolved and then bring the mixture to a boil over medium heat. Reduce the heat to low and simmer for 15-30 minutes, stirring occasionally.

Step 4: To serve, combine the peach puree mixture with the tea. Add a fresh slice of peach and sprig of mint for garnish.

Sparkling Pear Green Tea Lemonade

Nothing is more exquisite than sipping a chilled glass of pear green tea lemonade on a hot summer's day. The combination of the fruity sweetness of pears, the delicate aroma of green tea, and the zingy tartness of lemon creates a unique flavor that could be likened to a delicate dance in your mouth. While people might reach for more sugary beverages, making this lighter treat is worth the effort, as its complexity never fails to soothe. Pear green tea lemonade truly embodies a beautiful experience that will linger throughout your entire day.

Ingredients:
This will make 2 servings.
1 ripe pear
1 lemon
6 ounces hot water (180 ml)
2 tablespoons honey (30 ml)
2 ounces loose-leaf green tea or 2 teabags of green tea (about 50 g for loose-leaf)
sparkling water to top
2 sprigs mint
ice

Steps:

Step 1: Place green tea leaves in a cup or mug. Pour in the hot water and let steep for 3 to 5 minutes to extract the flavor.

Step 2: Meanwhile, peel and chop the pear into small pieces. Add the pear pieces to a blender with the lemon juice and honey. Blend until smooth.

Step 3: Once the green tea has finished steeping, strain the leaves and discard them.

Step 4: In a large pitcher or individual glasses, pour the tea and add in the pear lemonade mixture. Stir to combine. Top up the pitcher with sparkling water to give your lemonade a delightful fizz.

Step 5: Serve with ice cubes and garnish with mint.

Taro Milk Tea

Taro is a vegetable that is known for its beautiful and intricate purple hue, as well as its velvety texture. Its creamy, smooth texture when cooked makes it an ideal accompaniment to many different dishes from all cuisines. In many Asian cuisines, taro is most commonly found cooked into soups or stews, boiled alongside other vegetables or turned into unique dessert treats such as cakes and puddings.

Ingredients:
This will make 2 servings.
2 cups milk of choice (about 475 ml)
1 cup taro (150 g) *or* 2–3 tablespoons powdered taro (30–40 ml)
¼ cup sugar (50 g)
1–2 tablespoons black tea or two teabags (15–30 g)
2 cups water (for brewing tea, about 475 ml)

Steps:

Step 1: Start by brewing a pot of strong black tea. To do this, add the black tea or teabags to the boiling water, let it steep for 3 to 5 minutes, then set aside.

Step 2: For fresh taro—peel and chop one medium taro root into small pieces. In a pot, add the taro with water and bring to a boil for about 10 minutes until the taro is softened. Once softened, add the taro root to a blender with one cup of milk and blend until smooth. Combine with the brewed black tea to the mixture.

If you are using the powder form, simply mix the powder with the brewed tea.

Step 3: Sweeten the tea to taste with honey or sugar, then serve hot or cold.

Goodbye for Now

As we come to the end of this charming picnic book, I would like to take a moment to reflect on our journey. I hope that these tips and suggestions have helped you create unforgettable picnics of your own. There are no limits to the joys of picnicking—whether you're gathering with friends and family, enjoying a romantic outing with your significant other, or simply savoring some time alone in nature.

This extends far beyond the confines of a traditional picnic basket. It's a celebration of nature, an opportunity to reconnect with our surroundings and each other. Whether you're lazing on a blanket in the park, perched atop a mountain peak, or simply savoring a sandwich outdoors, you can enjoy a little escape at any time.

I urge you to take a step outside and enjoy the beauty of the world around you. Discover your own favorite picnic spots and recipes, and make every day a celebration of life's simple pleasures. With an open heart and a curious mind, the possibilities for a perfect picnic are truly endless. Thank you again for joining me on this journey.

Thank You

This book would not be possible without the following:

To my cherished online family: It is in our shared space that I've found a home for my passion. Your constant support has been the very heart of this cookbook. To each of you who've liked, shared, and tried my recipes, this book is a tribute to our journey together.

To my parents, Fernando and Sok Wa: It's in your loving guidance that I learned the magic of turning ingredients into memories.

Mei and Gabriel, my cherished in-laws: Thank you for opening your kitchen and hearts to me. By welcoming me, you've not only shared recipes but also moments of joy, laughter, and love.

To my beloved Aaron: Behind every dish I've crafted, every recipe I've penned, and every challenge I've faced, there's been a constant force of love, support, and belief—and that's you. Your unwavering faith in me has been the cornerstone of this cookbook and the journey leading to it.

To Max: In every chapter of my life, and now this cookbook, your insights and wisdom have been a guiding light. More than just the edits and revisions, it's your friendship that has encouraged me to finish.

To all who have played a part, no matter how big or small, in the making of this cookbook—I am deeply grateful. May these recipes bring as much joy to your picnic as they have to mine.

About the Author

Cristina Viseu is a content creator with a love for crafting beautiful and delicious dishes. She's garnered a loyal following on social media, captivating audiences with her easy-to-follow recipes, curated food recommendations, and picturesque picnics. Rooted in the belief that good food should be as delightful to the eyes as it is to the palate, Cristina emphasizes that creating a memorable dining experience can be both simple and attainable, transforming any occasion into something truly special.

Mango Publishing, established in 2014, publishes an eclectic list of books by diverse authors—both new and established voices—on topics ranging from business, personal growth, women's empowerment, LGBTQ studies, health, and spirituality to history, popular culture, time management, decluttering, lifestyle, mental wellness, aging, and sustainable living. We were named 2019 *and* 2020's #1 fastest growing independent publisher by *Publishers Weekly*. Our success is driven by our main goal, which is to publish high-quality books that will entertain readers as well as make a positive difference in their lives.

Our readers are our most important resource; we value your input, suggestions, and ideas. We'd love to hear from you—after all, we are publishing books for you!

Please stay in touch with us and follow us at:

Facebook: Mango Publishing
Twitter: @MangoPublishing
Instagram: @MangoPublishing
LinkedIn: Mango Publishing
Pinterest: Mango Publishing
Newsletter: mangopublishinggroup.com/newsletter

Join us on Mango's journey to reinvent publishing, one book at a time.